SPEAK OUT
AND HELP HER RECOVER

Stories Of Hope And Healing For Survivors Of Gender-Based Violence

Compiled by

AMANDA WILLETT

AUTHORS:

Angela Baltkois, Esther Enyolu, Tiwonge Gondwe, Mary Anne Gronningen, Erin Crawford Hellier, Rachel Lee, Sarah Lewis, Beatrice Chisomo Mateyo, Martha Mills, Audrey Monette, Dawn Nickel, Jodi Pugh, Jenny Ross

Published by Rituals for Recovery, 2024

SPEAK OUT AND HELP HER RECOVER: STORIES OF HOPE AND HEALING FOR SURVIVORS OF GENDER-BASED VIOLENCE

© 2024 by Angela Baltkois, Esther Enyolu, Tiwonge Gondwe, Mary Anne Gronningen, Erin Crawford Hellier, Rachel Lee, Sarah Lewis, Beatrice Chisomo Mateyo, Martha Mills, Audrey Monette, Dawn Nickel, Jodi Pugh, Jenny Ross, and Amanda Willett

All rights reserved. No portion of this book may be reproduced, stored in a retrieval system, or transmitted in any form by any means –electronic, mechanical, photocopy, recording, scanning, or other—except for brief quotations in critical reviews or articles, without the prior written permission of the publisher.

The manifesto on page 10 is adapted from these sources:
Yogis in Service and Cook-Cottone et al., (2016). Growth Zone
The Yogis in Service Team partnered with the University at Buffalo to create the YIS 12 Principles for Growth (see Catherine Cook-Cottone, Ph.D.'s and Wendy Guyker, Ph.D.'s Research Team;
(http://gse.buffalo.edu/about/directory/faculty/cook-cottone).

Published in Ontario Canada by Rituals for Recovery

ISBN: 978-1-7387834-4-1 (Paperback)
ISBN: 978-1-7387834-3-4 (Hardcover Book)
ISBN: 978-1-7387834-2-7 (Electronic Book)
ISBN: 978-1-7387834-1-0 (Digital)
ISBN: 978-1-7387834-0-3 (Audio)

DISCLAIMER
This is a work of nonfiction, but names may have been changed although no characters have been invented and no events fabricated. This book is not offering medical advice but presenting the perspectives of the authors. What has worked for them may or may not work for you. You should always contact a medical professional for medical advice.

www.ritualsforrecovery.com

DEDICATION

This book is dedicated to all survivors of gender-based violence, whose strength, resilience, and courage inspire us to speak out and work tirelessly for a world where such violence has no place.

To the survivors who found the strength to share their stories, you are beacons of hope, and your voices are a powerful force for change. Your courage shines a light on the path to healing and justice, guiding others toward a brighter future.

To the advocates, allies, and supporters who stand beside survivors, your unwavering commitment to ending gender-based violence is both noble and invaluable. Your dedication gives survivors the strength to speak out and helps us all on the journey toward a safer, more equitable world.

May this book serve as a testament to the resilience of survivors and a call to action for all those who believe in a world free from violence, discrimination, and fear.

Together, we can make a difference.

CONTENTS

INTRODUCTION by Amanda 1

**BEATRICE CHISOMO MATEYO: Hiking & Dancing My
   Way to Peace** 13
      EMPOWERMENT Principle 1: I CAN

RACHEL LEE: Everything for a Reason 29
      WORTH Principle 2: I AM WORTH THE EFFORT

JODI PUGH: Starting Over … Again 49
      SAFETY Principle 3: I DESERVE TO BE SAFE

MARTHA MILLS: Unfreezing 71
      BREATH Principle 4: MY BREATH IS MY MOST
      POWERFUL TOOL

ANGELA BALTKOIS: The Truth 91
      PRESENCE Principle 5: I AM WORKING TOWARDS
      PRESENCE IN MY BODY

**ERIN CRAWFORD HELLIER: Surviving an Olympic-Level
   Narcissist** 113
      FEELING Principle 6: I FEEL SO THAT I CAN HEAL

**TIWONGE GONDWE: From Shame and Poverty to International
   Respect** 135
      CHOICE Principle 7: I CAN FIND CHOICE IN
      THE PRESENT MOMENT

DAWN NICKEL: Recovering Out Loud 151

  GROUNDING Principle 8: MY BODY IS A SOURCE FOR
  CONNECTION, GUIDANCE, AND COPING

**AUDREY MONETTE: I Was Only Fifteen: A Journey to Surviving
Domestic Violence as a Teenager** 167

  OWNERSHIP Principle 9: I CAN CREATE THE CONDITIONS
  FOR SAFETY AND GROWTH

**MARY ANNE GRONNINGEN: Emerging from Pain Through
Love and a Life of Service** 193

  SUSTAINABILITY Principle 10: I CAN CREATE A BALANCE
  BETWEEN STRUCTURE AND CHANGE

SARAH LEWIS: Keep Using Your Voice 215

  COMPASSION Principle 11: I HONOR THE INDIVIDUAL
  PATH OF RECOVERY AND GROWTH

**JENNY ROSS: Shattered Illusions: From Fairy Tale Family to
Mental Health Domestic Nightmare** 241

  SELF-DETERMINATION Principle 12: I WORK TOWARD
  THE POSSIBILITY OF EFFECTIVENESS AND GROWTH
  IN MY OWN LIFE

**ESTHER ENYOLU: Supporting and Empowering Women and
Children with Lived Experiences of Violence and Abuse** 261

  COMMUNITY Principle 13: I AM SURROUNDED WITH A
  CIRCLE OF LOVE AND LIGHT

Divine Woman, Poem by Sarah Lewis 281

Resources 285
Acknowledgements 307
About Amanda Willett 309

INTRODUCTION

by Amanda Willett,
Director of Rituals for Recovery

Embracing Healing: The Story Behind Rituals for Recovery

In the quiet corners of our society, where shadows often obscure the truth beneath the veil of whispered stories and unspoken pain, there lies an untold narrative. It's a narrative of strength born from the crucible of complex trauma and the depths of gender-based violence. It's a story of resilience, hope, and the unwavering human spirit's power to not only endure but to rise above.

Survivor of Complex PTSD, Trauma, and Gender-Based Violence

> *"Complex trauma is exposure to varied and multiple traumatic events, defined as chronic, often of an invasive, interpersonal nature that begin early in life." Complex PTSD, also known as CPTSD, can result if a person experiences prolonged or repeated trauma over months or years, particularly due to childhood abuse or domestic violence.*

My journey as a survivor began in the aftermath of profound suffering from complex trauma, PTSD, and the insidious grip of gender-based violence which cast a long shadow over my life.

The scars were not only physical but emotional, etched deep into the recesses of my soul. The path to recovery seemed treacherous and uncertain, but throughout this challenging journey, I found guidance and support from mentors who played an integral role in my post-traumatic growth. These mentors include Dr. William Ammons who helped me navigate the complexities of PTSD and trauma recovery as well as Catherine Cook-Cottone, Sean Corne, Ashley Turner, Crystal Andrus Morrisette, Tony Robbins, Oprah, and Danielle Laporte, among others, who offered wisdom, inspiration, and tools for healing. They all were fundamental to my transformation.

Finding Healing and Empowerment

In the tapestry of life, each thread represents a unique journey, a path filled with triumphs, trials, and transformation. Mine was a voyage marked by valleys of despair and peaks of hope, and throughout it all, I discovered the incredible power of rituals in healing. Rituals offered solace, comfort, and a sense of control over a life that had often felt uncontrollable.

These were not grand gestures but simple, daily practices that became my lifeline. More than just symbolic gestures; they are profound tools that provide structure, meaning, and relief during the turbulent storms of recovery, creating a sense of stability in a world that often feels chaotic.

I stand before you today as a survivor, a testament to the human spirit's remarkable capacity to transcend suffering, find healing, and emerge from the darkest of places into the light of empowerment. My personal journey from silence to empowerment is a path that led me to break free from the cycle of complex trauma, to seek healing, and to find strength not only in my own recovery but in extending a hand to others who have suffered in silence.

Understanding Trauma: A Multifaceted Challenge

"Trauma creates change you do not choose. Healing creates changes you do choose."

Trauma can manifest in various forms, from physical injuries to emotional wounds, each carrying its unique burden. These experiences often disrupt the delicate balance between mind and body, leading to a cascade of distressing symptoms. To address trauma comprehensively, it's essential to adopt a holistic approach that engages both mental and physical dimensions.

The Healing Power of Rituals and Daily Practices for Mind-Body Wellness: A Holistic Approach to Trauma Recovery

In the realm of holistic well-being, the synergy between the mind and body is a potent force for healing. Trauma, whether physical or psychological, can leave enduring scars that permeate both our mental and physical landscapes.

The integration of rituals and daily practices into trauma recovery offers a holistic approach that harmonizes the mind and body. Whether through bottom-up methods like yoga or top-down strategies like mindfulness, these practices empower individuals to heal, fostering resilience and promoting overall wellness. By acknowledging the mind-body connection, we unlock the transformative potential of rituals in the journey towards healing and recovery.

At the end of each chapter, we delve into the influence of rituals and daily practices on trauma recovery, exploring both bottom-up and top-down approaches. You will be introduced to thirteen Principles of Growth and the power of rituals through affirmation, mindful focusing, meditation and somatic movement. My hope is that they offer you sacred space for introspection, growth, and connection.

The Birth of Rituals for Recovery

Through my healing process, I realized that I was not alone and that was a turning point in my journey. So many others carried the weight of their own stories, their own pain. It was this awareness that gave birth to RitualsForRecovery.com, a non-profit organization founded on the principles of compassion, healing, and community, dedicated to providing a safe space for survivors and a path toward recovery.

Our mission is to provide resources, support, and a community of resilience. Strengthening communities and supporting recovery through trauma-informed practices, training, and quality integrated care. We are committed to combatting complex trauma and the stigma and suffering that surrounds it. We believe that healing can be an art, a daily practice, and a ritual. We support helping professionals and human service organizations across the country to incorporate (TRMBW™) Trauma Responsive Mind Body Wellness & Social Emotional Learning (SEL) into their work with trauma survivors. Through the teachings of "Trauma Responsive Mind Body Wellness," we share the power of rituals and how those small, daily practices can bring healing and solace to those who have endured the unimaginable.

Our vision is a trauma-informed world with systems and networks of recovery and prevention; where healing and hope for a future in which equality, justice, inclusion, and harmony are the new normal for all.

The Help Her Recover Project

Within the framework of RitualsforRecovery.com, the Help Her Recover project took shape. Its purpose: to provide trauma relief and support to our community's survivors of gender-based violence. It was a way to extend a hand to those who, like me, had once felt alone in their struggle.

The Help Her Recover Project is a call to action to address violence against women, demand equity and promote good health and wellbeing. Millions of women and girls and Two Spirit, trans and non-binary people are at highest risk of experiencing gender-based violence.

Understanding the Prevalence: Statistics

The World Health Organization and Canada's Public Health Agency recognize gender-based violence as a significant public health issue. There is no question: violence affects mental health, which in turn affects all elements of health and wellbeing.

To truly comprehend the gravity of the issue, we must confront the statistics:

According to the United Nations, one in three women globally has experienced physical or sexual violence in their lifetime. For women of color or indigenous women that number is even higher.

The World Health Organization estimates that thirty-five of women have experienced either physical or sexual intimate partner violence or non-partner sexual violence.

Gender-based violence knows no boundaries; it affects people of all ages, backgrounds, and identities.

Dispelling Myths

Myth 1: "Gender-based violence only involves physical abuse." In reality, it encompasses various forms, including emotional, verbal, financial, and sexual abuse.

Myth 2: "It only happens in certain communities or cultures." Gender-based violence occurs worldwide, transcending cultural and geographical boundaries.

Myth 3: "Victims are to blame." No one asks for or deserves abuse. Blaming the victim perpetuates a culture of silence.

3. Emerging Trends

Gender-based violence is not static; it evolves with societal changes. With the rise of technology, cyberbullying and online harassment have become new forms of abuse. Additionally, the COVID-19 pandemic has intensified the problem, as lockdowns trapped many victims with their abusers.

4. Prevention Strategies

Prevention begins with education and awareness. We must teach respect, consent, and healthy relationships from an early age. Employers and organizations should implement policies to address and prevent workplace harassment. Legal reforms and enforcement are also essential steps.

5. Allyship and Support

Allyship plays a pivotal role in addressing gender-based violence. Support survivors by believing their stories, offering assistance without judgment, and being a source of emotional support. Remember that your actions as an ally can empower survivors to seek help.

6. Resources for Support

List National Resources Including RfR

> *"The promotion, protection and restoration of mental health and wellbeing is vital to collective healing and community capacity building. Critical supports need to be strengthened for abuse survivors experiencing mental health concerns, both to prevent and address violence." Amanda Willett, Founder, Rituals for Recovery.*

The Journey Continues

The Help Her Recover Project is our signature project that will bring the message of awareness of the impact of complex trauma to people around the world through the publication of this book: Speak Out and Help Her Recover, a high-profile awareness campaign across Canada, and a hybrid international conference.

Our Project Goals

Through strategic partnerships we will jointly coordinate community events, awareness walks, rallies, and fundraising initiatives to:

- Raise awareness and encourage survivors to seek help.
- Deliver trauma Informed education and trauma responsive training to healthcare professionals, first-responders, and social good industry practitioners.
- Engage community service providers with prevention tools, trauma responsive framework implementation, protocol, and policy development to increase the availability and quality of trauma-informed care.
- Provide access to peer learning, leadership and empowerment opportunities for marginalized women and girls.
- Share community support resources.

THE STORIES

Speak Out and Help Her Recover: Stories of Hope and Healing for Survivors of Gender-Based Violence

I am honored to introduce you to a collection of voices that have emerged from the shadows of suffering, the collective narrative of survivors, leaders, and advocates. Together, we have turned our pain into power, our suffering into a lifeline for others.

This book, *Speak Out and Help Her Recover: Stories of Hope and Healing for Survivors of Gender-Based Violence,* is not just a compilation of stories; it is a testament to the transformative power of sharing, connecting, and healing.

In a world often shrouded in silence and shadows, the pages of this book bear witness to the courageous voices that refuse to be stifled. This book is a profound testament to the indomitable spirit of women who have faced the darkest of trials and emerged as beacons of strength.

Within these chapters, the narratives of Angela Baltkois, Esther Enyolu, Tiwonge Gondwe, Mary Anne Gronningen, Erin Crawford Hellier, Rachel Lee, Sarah Lewis, Beatrice Chisomo Mateyo, Martha Mills, Audrey Monette, Dawn Nickel, Jodi Pugh, Jenny Ross converge, revealing the painful, yet resolute journeys they have undertaken. These women invite you to walk beside them as they bear their hearts and souls.

Their stories, each a mosaic of resilience, shine light on the myriad forms of gender-based violence, from the insidious clutches of domestic abuse to the harrowing ordeal of sexual assault. Through their words, we gain insight into the profound impact such violence inflicts upon individuals, families, and communities.

Yet, within the depths of their experiences, there exists a common thread—a testament to the human spirit's unyielding tenacity. These women have found the strength to reclaim their power, to rebuild what was shattered, and to heal what was broken. Their stories are not just stories; they are lifelines of hope, extended to those who have endured similar trials and to those who stand beside them in solidarity.

This book is more than just a compilation of accounts; it is a clarion call for change. It calls upon society to rise against gender-based violence in all its forms and manifestations, to raise awareness, and to provide unwavering support to those in need. It is a powerful reminder that healing, and recovery are not mere dreams but attainable realities, given the right resources and compassion.

As you embark on this poignant journey through the pages of *Speak Out and Help Her Recover*, you will bear witness to the strength, resilience, and hope that arise from the darkest of circumstances. These stories are a testament to the unbreakable spirit of survivors, a beacon guiding us toward a future where gender-based violence is eradicated once and for all. As we turn the pages, may you find inspiration, courage, and a renewed sense of purpose.

This book is a call to action. It's an invitation to stand with survivors, to speak out against gender-based violence, and to help her recover. Together let us embark on a journey from survivorship to empowerment, one ritual at a time, one story at a time. The journey begins here.

13 Principles and Affirmations to Help Her Recover

EMPOWERMENT
Principle 1: I CAN

WORTH
Principle 2: I AM WORTH THE EFFORT

SAFETY
Principle 3: I DESERVE TO BE SAFE

BREATH
Principle 4: MY BREATH IS MY MOST POWERFUL TOOL

PRESENCE
Principle 5: I WORK TOWARD PRESENCE IN MY BODY

FEELING
Principle 6: I FEEL SO THAT I CAN HEAL

CHOICE
Principle 7: I CAN FIND CHOICE IN THE PRESENT MOMENT

GROUNDING
Principle 8: MY BODY IS A SOURCE FOR CONNECTION, GUIDANCE, AND COPING

OWNERSHIP
Principle 9: I CAN CREATE THE CONDITIONS FOR SAFETY AND GROWTH

SUSTAINABILITY
Principle 10: I CAN CREATE A BALANCE BETWEEN STRUCTURE AND CHANGE

COMPASSION
Principle 11: I HONOR THE INDIVIDUAL PATH OF RECOVERY AND GROWTH

SELF-DETERMINATION
Principle 12: I WORK TOWARD THE POSSIBILITY OF EFFECTIVENESS AND GROWTH IN MY OWN LIFE

COMMUNITY
Principal 13: I AM SURROUNDED WITH A CIRCLE OF LIGHT AND LOVE

FOR CREDITS, SEE PAGE 2

SPEAK OUT

BEATRICE MATEYO

Beatrice is a Malawian human rights defender and co-founder of the Coalition for the Empowerment of Women and Girls (CEWAG). As an executive director and feminist, she works to raise awareness about gender-based violence (GBV) and empower women and girls with information to prevent it.

Beatrice shares her story of raped and intimate partner violence to help other survivors recover; her aim is that no woman or girl has to experience what she went through. She also creates linkages with other service providers and supports survivors in accessing necessary services. Beatrice lives in Malawi where she is surrounded by her
children and grandchildren.

HIKING & DANCING MY WAY TO PEACE

By
Beatrice Chisomo Mateyo

*I tell my story, not because it is unique, but because it is not.
It is the story of many girls.*

—Malala Yousafzai

I come from a blended middle-class family. I am the third-born of four girls and one boy. My parents worked full time which meant they left home in the early morning and would only return in the evening. During the day, the homestead was usually maintained by the maid and the garden boy. This was similar to other households in my small community in Malawi. And just like in similar communities all over the world, my siblings and I would go out to play in the afternoons after school. I was a jovial child and loved to play tag and soccer with my buddies as we waited for our parents to come home.

One hot summer afternoon, I was tired, so instead of going to play with the others, I was laying in my bed napping after school. I was ten years old and only myself and the houseboy were at home. I was in my bed facing the wall and woke up with a start when I felt someone touch my waist from behind. It was the houseboy. He forced himself on me.

After he was done, he threatened me, telling me he would harm me further if I told. He added that no one would believe me anyway.

I continued laying there in my bed after he left, unaware of the time, asking myself so many questions I couldn't get answers to. What just happened? Do I tell anyone, my mom, or my sisters? What do I say to them? How do I even begin? What will they think of me? Did I do something to invite him? My ten-year-old brain was struggling with the words to describe this incident to myself. I took a bath thinking that I could wash away the feeling of pain and the nausea I felt. I figured if I was clean, if I could wash away the incident, maybe I could forget it ever happened.

By nightfall, I was still silent, my head full of wondering what to do but nobody—not my sisters, brothers, mother, or adoptive father—noticed my despair. I wanted someone to say something, to see me and be able to tell something was wrong, that something was different. At the same time I had no idea what I'd say if I was confronted by anyone in my family. The idea "why should I bother to tell anyone" floated up into my head. I went to sleep in the same bed where it happened, and I woke up the next day. I remember standing near my mother, begging her with my soul to ask me what is wrong, hoping she would notice I was sad and quiet, but she did not. She was getting the household ready for the day and herself ready for work. She did not ask me anything that allowed me to try to explain. Instead, I went to school as usual.

The next few days went by slowly. The houseboy stared at me often and caught my eye a few times. He gave me a knowing look as if he approved my silence. I ignore him and the discomfort of being around him. Luckily, he was fired a few months later and I had made sure to never be at home alone with him, thus he never got the chance to do it again. I was relieved when he was gone, but the questions did not stop. I still sought out opportunities to tell my mother, but none came. There is no opening for a conversation like the one I wanted so I told myself to forget what happened. And time marched on.

I got married at age twenty-two when I was pregnant with our first child. It was an abusive marriage from the start; he regularly had affairs with other women. But this was married life and I assumed it was not very different from other marriages, although it was so different to what I expected. But I was not earning enough to sustain myself and now we had a child. He continued to humiliate me with his cheating, and I lost myself and my self-esteem in the process of just living and caring for our child.

I was in a really dark place. I couldn't bring myself to leave him because my livelihood was dependent on him, and he knew that. I spent most of my nights crying and thinking of ways to make myself better so he might love me more, and of fantastical ways of obtaining money so I could create a good life without the need for his financial support, but really, there was no hope in sight.

A few years later, I got pregnant again and our second born daughter was born. Despite my loyalty, he questioned the paternity of our daughter. I guess because of how he treated me, he was sure I must also be cheating, but I was not. I realized that his accusations and anger were ways of making sure he had control over me. I wanted to get out of the marriage, but he threatened to "deal" with my children if I even tried. I was never even sure what he meant, but I didn't want to find out, so I stayed. Eventually, it got too much. While he was away, I snuck the children out to my sister in a nearby district before he got back. I left.

I met the man who would become my second husband a few years after my divorce. He was kind, loving, and all a girl could have wanted. He adored my children and gave them all the love and support we needed. I felt so lucky to have a second chance and felt we could create a good family life together. His kindness meant my children were developing a sense of belonging in the home we created with him, as was I. However, this only lasted a short while. I realized his loving behavior was perhaps only a honeymoon phase but I kept trying, hopeful even as he started showing his true colors. He started questioning my every move, wanting to know where I was going, who I was meeting, and why.

At first, I took his possessiveness as a sign of love towards me. We got married and I thought agreeing to marry him was a way of showing my commitment, but getting married only made it worse. I was expected to be more subservient because of the ceremony that we had in church. I had my third child, our first together, a few years after we got married and I thought that would serve to reassure him, but it did not. He became more controlling and violent towards me. I thought to myself that if I became yet more subservient then maybe my husband would be more tolerant of me. But it turned out that the more I was subservient, the more he was controlling and violent towards me.

I couldn't take it anymore and decided to leave. However, I felt that I would be judged because this was my second marriage and everyone would definitely think that there had to be something wrong with me to have two failed marriages, so instead I stayed. I blamed myself even though I tried so hard to appease my husband through subservience even while I worked outside of the home to bring in money. At the time, I was working with a small organization, part of the church, which was helping women who were in violent relationships. Our organization empowered women and helped them to leave. Despite my job, I didn't see myself as in the same shoes as our clients. I had obtained the job because it was available—I was not yet an activist. Because of what was happening at home, it was like I did the work without noticing the irony of me preaching to women that they must love themselves enough to leave and take care of their children, yet not doing it myself.

I was settling a woman into a lovely new home after having helped her leave a bad relationship and she showed me such appreciation that I considered how good I was at my job. I saw her children's safe and colorful bedroom and thought of the turbulence my own children were in. It finally dawned on me that I could not help other women to leave violent situations while staying in one myself. I saw it was possible to create a better life as I was helping other women do it. I was telling them that they were not to blame and helping them to discard feelings of shame. Soon enough, I got the courage coupled with enough irritation at his behavior to make a move. I couldn't take living with him for a moment longer, so I took my children and left him.

I was approaching forty and feeling confused about my future. I had a great disappointment in myself. My husband told me no one would want me and this was eating me up, especially as he had cheated so much and I felt like nothing. My previous husband had said the same. I took up drinking more than usual just to numb the pain. I also started sleeping with random men just to validate myself, feeling like their brief attentions would be enough to enable me to gain my self-worth because both my previous husbands had made me feel so worthless and not deserving of love. My life experience with violence and abuse was eating me up inside and affecting my work and my whole frame of mind.

On my fortieth birthday, several of my closest female friends invited me to a lovely restaurant to celebrate me. I didn't feel worth celebrating, despite how well I applied my makeup, despite the compliments about my lovely outfit with high heeled-shoes, and despite the brightness of my smile. I greeted each friend with a hug and feigned excitement while my heart was breaking inside of me. Before long, I could not control my sadness; my eyes welled up with tears. On my birthday surrounded by loving friends, I cried in that lovely restaurant. I opened up and told them of my abusive marriages and of the secret I had never before revealed: I told them I was raped at age ten by the servant. I felt such relief when I let go of that horrible secret. I was afraid to raise my eyes to meet theirs.

I was overwhelmed with the love they showed me and their acceptance, rather than the rejection my childish mind almost expected. Of course, my friends would love me even more when they were witnesses to what I'd had to suppress for so long. What surprised me, however, is that each of the women had a similar story of gender-based violence that they themselves were burying. Secrets that were also eating them up inside.

Being able to talk about my pain was like getting a load off my shoulders. Being able to help my friends as they released their own pain was a gift I received for the bravery of sharing my story. Although we talked about our traumatic experiences, there wasn't anyone in the room that had hope or any solutions to deal with their traumas. But at least we had taken that first step: we were no longer holding the secrets of our abusers. We had released something and there was the chance for healing to start.

Shortly after this, a friend of mine who attended the dinner introduced me to jogging as a way of losing weight. Little did I know that this would lead me to a journey of healing from my past pain and trauma. Through jogging I felt myself gaining strength. Through jogging and the controlled breathing and stamina I was developing, I found ways of controlling the thoughts that had previously overwhelmed me. I found myself proud of my abilities and I joined a jogging group.

Once I joined this group, I started to feel a sense of love and kindness towards myself. I found that this shared love of jogging brought me in touch with people I admired and who welcomed me. I was getting more and more positive feelings in my life, and they were pushing the feelings of self-hate away. I felt such relief as my pride in my growing strength, in my new community, in the new activities I was part of were making me think of other things rather than the words of my husbands, and the details of each past trauma.

I had occasionally hiked the local hills and some mountains, but now I was more purposeful in my growing desire for a connection to nature. It was like being in the beauty of the natural world reassured me of my value. I saw myself as part of the beauty of nature, and just as the trees, grasses, birds, and other animals were creatures of nature, so was I. I could love my power as my feet hit the paths and raised the beautiful red dust that is characteristic of our area around me. I loved the feeling of the sun on my skin and the warmth of it on my head as I hiked up through the mountains.

I cannot escape from the fact that sometimes I am reminded of the evil that is gender-based violence because I still work in the same sector helping women and girls overcome the issues that they are facing in their lives. However, what I have found most effective in helping me find myself is the love that I have found in movement. I introduced my daughters to hiking and jogging, and together we found so much joy, but our favorite type of movement is dancing. Now part of my rituals for recovery includes a love of dance with other women and particularly my daughters. The exuberance of shaking our bodies to the rhythm of music, and the firmness of pounding our feet on the Earth, connects me through the artistry of music, and the bonds of my love of my daughters and other women.

Through this I have learnt the expression of unconditional love and I know that I am able to move past what happened to me. There is a lot of victim-blaming in my society but if one learns to move past all that and focus on yourself, you can heal and shut out the voices that paint you with blame and try to cover you in shame.

Through my own personal trauma, I have been able to start an organization that helps to raise awareness on GBV and provides awareness on available avenues for survivors of GBV. I do hope that sharing my story here within this book will help people. The ease of simply going outside and putting your face up to the sun can do a lot to ease the mind. I hope that in sharing I can inspire others and help them to release their pain through removing the burden of secrets. Through opening up and risking being vulnerable despite the prevalence of victim-blaming, I have helped others to also open up. We are healing. I wish the same for others.

Help Her RECOVER

> The most common way people give up their power is by thinking they don't have any.
>
> ~ *Alice Walker*

Help Her RECOVER

By Amanda Willett

EMPOWERMENT Principle 1: "I CAN," is a fundamental theme in the recovery from gender-based violence. Survivors of such violence often face feelings of powerlessness, fear, and trauma. This principle underscores the essential concept that survivors can regain their sense of agency, self-worth, and control over their lives. Recovery begins with the realization that, despite the trauma endured, survivors possess the inherent capability to reclaim their autonomy and make choices that contribute to their healing journey.

Empowerment is not only about personal growth but also about advocating for systemic changes that address gender-based violence and promote a safer, more equitable society for all. This principle inspires survivors to embark on a path toward healing and transformation, reaffirming their resilience and capacity to overcome the challenges they face.

Beatrice Mateyo's journey is a testament to her resilience, self-discovery, and her ability to overcome trauma and adversity. Her story begins with her childhood in a middle-class family in Malawi, where she experienced a traumatic incident of sexual abuse by the houseboy at the age of ten. This traumatic event left her with profound questions and emotional scars, yet she found herself unable to share her pain with her family due to fear, shame, and uncertainty about how to articulate her experience.

As Beatrice grew older, she entered an abusive marriage, marked by her husband's infidelity, control, and threats. Despite the hardships, she remained in the marriage due to economic dependency and fear for her children's safety. Her self-esteem dwindled, and she felt trapped in a cycle of violence.

It was through her work with an organization that assisted women in abusive relationships that Beatrice began to realize the need for self-love and empowerment. Although she was counseling other women to leave abusive situations, she had not yet taken the step herself. However, her experiences with helping others planted the seeds of change within her.

Beatrice's turning point came when she finally found the courage to leave her second abusive marriage. She overcame the stigma and self-blame she had carried for years, taking her children to safety. This decision marked her reclamation of power and self-worth.

On her fortieth birthday, Beatrice opened up to her friends about her traumatic past and experiences of abuse, including the childhood incident she had kept secret for so long. This act of vulnerability and sharing brought a wave of support and understanding from her friends, who themselves revealed their hidden stories of gender-based violence. It was a pivotal moment of healing and empowerment, demonstrating the strength of communal support.

Beatrice's healing journey continued as she discovered the transformative power of movement. Jogging and hiking became outlets for her emotional pain and sources of empowerment. She realized that connecting with nature and physical activity allowed her to reclaim her strength and self-worth.

Dance became a powerful symbol of empowerment and healing for Beatrice and her daughters. Through dance, they found joy, self-expression, and a bond that helped them overcome their shared trauma.

Beatrice's story also highlights her commitment to raising awareness about gender-based violence and providing support to survivors. She founded an organization to help survivors and educate the community about available resources.

In sharing her story, Beatrice hopes to inspire others to break the silence, release their pain, and find healing through self-discovery and empowerment. Her journey exemplifies the transformative power of resilience, self-love, and the support of a loving community.

In summary, Beatrice Mateyo's chapter beautifully illustrates how she transitioned from a victim to a survivor, embodying the theme of empowerment. Her story serves as a beacon of hope for others, encouraging them to realize their own strength and take steps toward healing and self-empowerment.

EMPOWERMENT

Principle 1:
I CAN

What makes me feel powerful?
What makes me feel calm?
What makes me feel in control?

Affirmation:

"I am strong. I am taking action on all the things I set out to do."

Mountain Pose: Tadasana
Tadasana arms and palms facing up to the sky

Stand with your feet slightly apart while keeping your feet balanced on both feet. Inhale and raise your arms above your head. Interlock your fingers with your palms facing up. Keep your gaze ahead. Exhale and raise your shoulders towards your ears. Rollback your shoulders and lower your spine while straightening your posture and opening your chest. Relax all your muscles. Return to the starting position.

Tadasana steps help in boosting your energy levels by rejuvenating your mind and body. This boosts your memory, focus, and concentration.

Mindful Focusing Meditation:

This practice is designed to help you tap into your inner strength and confidence. Find a quiet and comfortable place to sit or lie down, and let's begin:

Posture and Comfort:

Sit or lie down in a comfortable position. Keep your back straight, but not rigid, to allow for relaxed breathing. Place your hands on your lap or gently on your knees. Close your eyes if you're comfortable doing so.

Deep Breathing:

Begin by taking a few deep, cleansing breaths. Inhale slowly through your nose and exhale fully through your mouth. With each breath, imagine that you are inhaling positive energy and exhaling any tension or doubt.

Affirmation:

As you continue to breathe deeply and slowly, bring your attention to the affirmation, "I can." With each inhalation, silently say to yourself, "I." With each exhalation, say, "can." Visualize this affirmation as a bright, powerful light within you that grows stronger with each breath.

Body Scan:

Begin a gentle body scan, starting from the top of your head and moving down to your toes. As you focus on each body part, repeat the affirmation silently. For example, as you focus on your head, say, "I can." Move to the neck, shoulders, and so on, repeating the affirmation with intention.

Visualization:

Imagine a situation or challenge in your life where you may have doubts or feel disempowered. Visualize yourself confidently and successfully navigating this situation. See yourself taking positive actions and achieving your goals.

Gratitude:

Shift your focus to the things you are grateful for in your life. As you think of each one, say, "I can" in gratitude for the opportunities and blessings you have.

Return to the Breath:

Come back to your breath, focusing on the natural rhythm of your inhalations and exhalations. With each breath, affirm, "I can," reinforcing your inner strength and confidence.

Closing:

Take a few more deep breaths, slowly bringing your awareness back to the present moment.

When you're ready, open your eyes if they were closed. This mindful meditation practice can be repeated as often as you like, and you can adjust the duration to fit your schedule. It's a powerful way to remind yourself of your inner strength and ability to overcome challenges.

SPEAK OUT

RACHEL LEE

Rachel is a changemaker in the field of social work. She is committed to creating a safe and welcoming environment for radical healing and self-compassion. Utilizing theoretical knowledge from her trauma-informed yoga teacher training as well as her lived experience, she shares the effects of trauma and practical, whole-body/holistic steps to healing. She speaks about gender-based violence, intimate partner and domestic violence, drug and alcohol abuse, and sexual assault.

Rachel lives on the traditional territory of the Kwanlin Dün and Ta'an Kwäch'än First Nations in what is known as
Whitehorse, Yukon, Canada.

EVERYTHING FOR A REASON
By
Rachel Lee

Only when we are brave enough to explore the darkness will we discover the infinite power of our light.

—Brene Brown

The hardest decision I've had to make was the choice to have an abortion. For as long as I can remember, I've wanted to be a mother, yet when I was faced with the harsh reality that I was growing an innocent and precious life within me I knew I could not bring that tender soul into my violent and volatile reality. Deep inside me, the wisdom of my womanhood told me *now is not the time*, and I whispered to my unborn child *these are not the circumstances for you, my child*. I myself was a child, lost and confused in the death grip of addiction and violence.

My first relationship at seventeen was what you would expect from teenage love. It was clouded with fantasy, with hopes for being together forever. I dreamed I would marry my high school sweetheart. But the delusion quickly came to a halt and reality hit me hard. I was in love with someone who did not have the capacity to love me back, and frankly, I also did not have the capacity to love fully either.

My first boyfriend came from a family of intergenerational trauma stemming from the violence of the Canadian government against Indigenous people on Turtle Island, the name this land's original people call North America. The policy of taking Indigenous children away from their parents to "kill the Indian and save the man" started well before 1867 when Canada became a nation. It was Canada's first leader who cemented the devastating residential school system into Canada's constitution. Children were forcibly removed from their families and communities into boarding schools riddled with mental, emotional, physical, sexual, and spiritual violence. Many children never saw home or their families again. Those who made it out of the prison of their childhood were faced with incredible hardship, racism and inequity spanning across generations.

His family took me in as their own; I had a special place and role as a partner and I was stepmother to his child, his parent's first grandchild. Our identities became entangled with each other, and our worlds collided. I, a privileged, middle class white girl becoming a woman, pursuing higher education; he, a marginalized Indigenous boy, becoming a man, who dropped out of high school when he had his first child.

Not a day goes by that I do not think of him, pray for him, and wish with all of my being that there was a possibility to be together in this life. We were each other's first love. I will always love him. He holds a piece of my heart forever. I will never regret my time with him, but that does not mean he did not hurt me. He introduced me to his world, which included poverty, addiction, drugs, gangs, violence, human trafficking. I'd known about all these dangers, but once I loved somebody who was in that world, where these were experiences not concepts but reality, my whole world was turned upside down.

His trauma led him to worm his way into my head and had me questioning everything about myself. He would manipulate me with mind games, confusing me because he said he loved me but was also doing terrible things throughout our four-year relationship. Towards the end, I found out he was cheating on me: he said he stopped counting how many times after he hit thirty. He took my virginity and was the only person I had been with throughout the entire relationship. As a young woman already struggling with confidence and body image, that shot me deep into a dark hole of depression. There were a few times he got physically aggressive with me, such as ripping my shirt from my body during a particularly bad fight. Eventually I had enough of being treated like that and finally had the courage and confidence to break up. But things got worse before they got better.

After the relationship ended, I started drinking and doing drugs to numb the pain. I was intoxicated more than I was sober. I spent my weeks waiting for the weekend because I knew I was going to get drunk and high. During the weekend, I would drink snort, smoke, and ingest all kinds of substances that were dangerous and even deadly in the right quantity and mix. I would get so fucked up I would black out and eventually lose consciousness.

I know of four times I was raped; it could be more, but I don't remember. One perpetrator told me they had the best sex of their life—with my unconscious body. So, I drank and used drugs to numb the pain that kept piling on.

On my twenty-third birthday, I was raped by my then boyfriend. I was black-out drunk and do not remember calling him or asking him to come pick me up. The next morning, I woke up naked in his bed and knew what had happened. There was a sinking feeling in my body. Again, I wondered: how someone who said they loved me could do such a vile thing to me? After getting half-dressed, I did a line of cocaine to numb my brain and body from the realization of how little I was cared about, how little I truly mattered to those around me.

I got to where I could not wait until the weekend for my next high; I started partying on weeknights, too. Going to work on a few hours of sleep—if I was lucky—still drunk and high from the night before.

By the grace of God, my concerned coworkers and friends told my boss, and I was presented with a way out: a ticket to rehab. But I refused it and was fired from my full-time permanent job. My pride and ego would not accept that I could be one of those people whose addiction was so bad I needed to be institutionalized. I knew I had a problem, but I was going to fix it my way, I decided. For better or for worse.

Ten months prior to this, I found out I was fifteen weeks pregnant. Something deep inside me knew I could not and would not have this baby. Her father was deeply involved in a gang and I was drinking and doing drugs throughout the entire pregnancy, even after I found out because I knew I would not keep her. Staying high was the only way I knew how to cope with the insurmountable pain of the decision I was making.

I felt stuck. Paralyzed by fear, knowing it was a disservice to me to keep the baby and petrified of the process. I had a surgical abortion at almost nineteen weeks of pregnancy. I flew from my small northern community in the Yukon to the city of Vancouver for the procedure. Because I was so far along, it was a two-day process. First, my cervix had to be dilated. That night was the worst pain of my life, or so I thought. The next day I went for the procedure. I was given drugs to induce labor and thirty minutes later I was in the chair, my legs in stirrups and a stranger in a mask was inserting a metal device inside me to abort the growing baby in my belly. That was the worst pain I have ever experienced. I went against everything my body was preparing for, yet I just knew it was what I had to do. The force that tells the flowers it is spring and time to bloom, that tells the tide when to rise and fall, was telling me to let this sweet, tender, and innocent baby go back to the spirit realm.

I was convinced I died on that table, and part of me did. The next day, I flew home and returned to my life as if nothing happened. I kept drinking and using drugs, but this time, rather than to just numb the pain, I also wanted to die. I was begging God to end my life. I was hoping I would take it too far and never wake up again. I prayed to be reunited with my baby girl, yet felt I deserved to live in this hell for my sin. The psychological torture I went through is inexplicable and otherworldly. I listened for a force greater than myself to stop going down this path. I cried and screamed and begged for a sign that someone or something was coming to save me. Little did I know that I would be the one to save myself.

I shamed myself: *how dare you call yourself a woman when you stopped what you are created for—you took the easy way out, you coward!* My inner critic consumed my being. Every waking moment was dominated by shame, guilt, and embarrassment for what I had done. So, I drank and drank and drank, every time praying to God that He would reclaim me.

But that didn't work. I woke up every time, hoping the next would be my last. Until one day I woke up feeling different. That morning, I decided this was not the life I was meant to live. I knew I did not sacrifice my baby in vain and that after all the pain, the blood, the lifetime of tears cried between the time I found out I was pregnant to the time I was no longer pregnant, I had to do something more. None of that was to be taken for granted. I could not keep returning to the same life I sacrificed my baby to get out of. It was not an option.

So, I kept going. Living. Even though I was living in hell for my sins, even though I still thought about all the ways I could die, I kept going. God reclaimed me; He gave me the strength to start the healing work. And it has been a long, hard journey but worth every moment of self-doubt, self-sabotage for the privilege to be alive and on this Earth.

I wonder what exactly was the catalyst event that set me on my path of healing. I think it was a series of events, of feeling like I didn't belong with the people I was around. Feeling and knowing I was put on this planet for more than drinking and drugging. And although having an abortion was the most difficult choice I've had to make, and the hardest thing I've ever done, I do not regret my choice and would do it again if I had to go back. It sent me on a dark path for a while where I truly believed I had died and woken up in hell, not a day going by without thinking about how I might die. But no matter how much I wished to be taken from this Earth, nothing happened. That is how I knew I was supposed to be here. So, I started the painstaking journey of making peace with my past.

The beginning of my healing journey was ugly. The days and nights blurred together as if I was in a time warp. I was plagued to feel every emotion I had stuffed deep down inside my psyche and being. I started to remember things I did not want to remember. I had visions of my unconscious body being raped. I had nightmares for years of chasing a crying baby but never getting to it in time, waking up with my jaw locked, shaking and sweating. I didn't get a full night's sleep for over three years, as I was plagued by night terrors of either rape or a crying baby in the abyss. I felt like there was a darkness following me, lurking around every corner, waiting for me, wanting to consume me.

Only once I stopped running away from the darkness that followed me and turned to face it did I realize it was the part of me, that the darkness was a protector. The part of me who knew I could not handle being conscious during rape, the part of me who knew no matter how hard it was going to be, I had to let my baby go for my future. The part of me who used drugs and alcohol to cope with the pain so I didn't kill myself. The darkness was not something to be feared, rather something to be thanked, loved, and accepted; the darkness was to be honored.

So, I started writing about the terrible things that happened to me and the more I wrote, the more at ease I felt with myself, the choices I made, and the things that happened to me. I said the affirmation "I am loved and lovable; I am safe and at home in my body; I am where, when, and who I am supposed to be." Slowly, I released my attachment to my identity as a victim and saw myself as a survivor.

Against all odds, I made it out of my entanglement with a hurt boy who needed to use violence and was part of a gang to feel worthy of respect. I had stepped out of the timeline where I was a university drop-out and a young single mother to an innocent and traumatized baby; I stepped away instead of repeating the cycle. I realized what I thought was the worst thing I could have done as a woman was actually an act of unconditional love for myself and my unborn baby. I knew both of us deserved better and I made the hardest choice a woman can make.

I let go of the what ifs: what if I made the wrong choice, what if he was going to change, what if we could be the family I dreamed for us? I wrote him a letter. I told him I would always love him, that he would always hold a piece of my heart. I told him we are living together as a happy and healthy family in another life, that I knew he had good inside of him and that he was just a little lost right now. I forgave him and started to move on. I hold him deep within my heart and we will always be connected, for we share a soul in the unseen realm. I forgave him for shattering my heart and soul into a million pieces and thank myself for picking up all of the pieces, one by one.

I started to turn my energy and attention toward myself and the things that light me up. Journaling, spending time in nature by the river that runs behind my childhood home, being in the presence of people I love and who love me back in the ways I deserve, somatic practices such as yoga and Pilates. I started to love my body again, to breathe, to speak kindly to myself, to move through life with grace. To acknowledge that I have been through hell, yet every day I wake up, I am grateful for another chance to spread love in this world.

Finally, I could see that good things were happening because everything happens for a reason. Yes, I made the one of the hardest decisions a woman faces. Yes, I was in the claws of drug and alcohol addiction. Yes, I was violated in the worst way, time and time again. Yes, I had lost many of my friends and nearly torn my entire family apart. Still, I knew, by the grace of God, I was here for a reason, and that reason is to tell my story.

The reasons I was able to do this are the people God sent to heal me. My incredible therapists who have laughed and cried with me as I open up and share parts of my story; my close friends from childhood and university who would wade courageously into my darkness to remind me of who I am and what I am capable of; my parents who sacrificed their lives so that I could live a better life than theirs; and my beloved sister, who I simply would not be here without, who always answered my calls when I was deep in suicidal ideation and told me everything will be okay. Despite how much I hurt her over the years, she loved me so fiercely that even when she hated me, she would drop what she was doing to make sure I was going to be okay. The love and kindness that was shown to me during my darkest days is what motivates me to keep trekking through the murky waters of life.

And now, as I write these words, I am in my last year of university getting a degree in social work. I am on my way to becoming a registered yoga teacher. I am healing my relationship with my family. I am deepening my relationships with my dear friends and mentors. I am writing about my story to share it with others who may be going through something similar or who may find inspiration in my words. I am sharing what was once my deepest, darkest secret. Sharing what once filled me with shame, embarrassment, and regret, and declaring it as an act of love.

You have power over your mind. You can control your thoughts and actions; you can change your beliefs about yourself. You can change your entire reality. It is not easy, but no one said life was going to be easy. Taking accountability for your thoughts and actions is a radical act of self love. The Buddha says life is suffering, but suffering occurs when we are attached to that which we identify with, whether it be a role, a title, the way we look. All of those attachments are superficial. We are pure light and energy in human form. We were made in the image of

God, the great creator and mystery of the Universe, and because His love for humanity runs so deep; He will always answer when called upon and show up in people and situations when you least expect but most need it. We can rest easy knowing we are unconditionally loved.

As I look back, I would never have imagined that I could have achieved what I have. And my wish for those who find themselves lost in a cycle of abuse is this: know that you are not broken. You are not unlovable or unworthy of being because of the things you've done or the things that have been done to you. You are a warrior, a gift from God, and you are meant to share your gifts and your story with the world. You are here for a reason. And I pray that you find that reason within your experiences.

Help Her RECOVER

You alone are enough.
You have nothing to
prove to anybody

~ *Maya Angelou*

Help Her RECOVER

By Amanda Willett

WORTH Principle 2: "I AM WORTH THE EFFORT," encapsulates a crucial theme in the recovery process from gender-based violence. Survivors often grapple with feelings of diminished self-worth, shame, and self-blame because of the violence they've endured. This principle reinforces the essential idea that every survivor inherently possesses immense worth and deserves to be treated with respect, dignity, and care. It encourages survivors to recognize that investing in their own well-being and healing journey is not just valid but imperative. Through therapy, support networks, and self-care practices, survivors can rebuild their self-esteem and self-compassion. The principle emphasizes that they are not defined by the violence inflicted upon them and that their lives are worth the effort it takes to recover, rediscover their sense of self, and ultimately thrive beyond their painful experiences. It's a reminder that, regardless of the past, they deserve a future filled with happiness, fulfillment, and a renewed sense of self-worth.

Rachel Lee's story is a powerful testament to the principle of self-worth and the profound strength that can emerge from even the most challenging circumstances. Rachel faced one of the most agonizing decisions a person can make: choosing to have an abortion due to a turbulent and unsafe environment. Her journey was marked by addiction, abusive relationships, and a deep sense of despair. However, throughout her narrative, Rachel's strength, and resilience shine through. She faced her darkest moments head-on, acknowledging her pain and her past. Despite the immense struggles she encountered, Rachel never lost sight of her worth and the potential for growth and healing within her.

Rachel's story is a salute to her unwavering determination to rise above her circumstances. She navigated a world of intergenerational trauma and abuse, ultimately choosing a path of self-preservation and love for herself and her unborn child. Her decision to have an abortion, though agonizing, was an act of self-compassion, recognizing that her child deserved a different life.

Through her narrative, Rachel demonstrates the power of gratitude and self-acceptance. She embraces her past, acknowledges her mistakes, and chooses to learn from them. Her journey is a testament to the transformative power of facing one's darkness, finding healing, and ultimately sharing her story as an act of love and empowerment.

In the end, Rachel's story embodies the essence of the WORTH Principle: recognizing that one is worth the effort to heal, grow, and create a better life. Her journey of self-discovery, forgiveness, and transformation serves as an inspiring example for others who may be navigating similar challenges. Rachel's message is clear: every individual has inherent worth, regardless of their past, and they are here for a reason—to share their unique gifts and stories with the world.

WORTH

Principle 2:
I AM WORTH THE EFFORT

How do I practice self-acceptance?
How do I advocate for myself?
How do I remind myself that I am enough?

Amanda Willett

RITUALS FOR Recovery

Affirmation:

I am capable, strong, worthy, and always enough. I am worthy of respect from myself and others. I fully love the person I am, both inside and out.

Try the Butterfly Hug to Help with PTSD Symptoms

The Butterfly Hug is an easy relaxation technique and self-soothing tool that can be used anywhere, at any time.

Sukhasana Easy Seated Pose-butterfly hug tapping. How to do the Butterfly Hug

1. First you want to find a comfortable, quiet location and sit up tall with your back straight.
2. Close or lower your eyes and start with some deep, purposeful breathing. Try breathing from your diaphragm if possible.
3. Notice any emotions or distress that may come up and just continue to breathe through it.
4. Cross your hands and place them on your chest so each middle finger rests right below the opposite collarbone. Fan your fingers, resting them on your chest and your thumbs will be pointed towards your chin.

5. You can interlock your thumbs, so it looks like a butterfly's body and the hands are its wings.
6. Now, you are going to alternate tapping your hands on your chest, slowly and rhythmically (left, right, left, right, etc.) for at least 8 rounds. Don't forget your deep breathing while you're fluttering your butterfly wings
7. Stop and check your level of distress. If your distress has not increased, try a couple more sets of 8. Stop after each set to check your level of distress, continuing if you are starting to feel less distress or more relaxed.

Mindful Focusing Meditation :

This practice will help you cultivate a strong sense of self-worth and self-compassion. Find a quiet and comfortable place to sit or lie down, and let's begin:

Posture and Comfort:

Sit or lie down in a comfortable position.
Keep your back straight, but not rigid, to allow for relaxed breathing. Place your hands on your lap or gently on your knees.
Close your eyes if you're comfortable doing so.

Centering Breath:

Begin by taking a few deep, calming breaths. Inhale deeply through your nose, allowing your abdomen to expand, and exhale slowly through your mouth, releasing any tension.

Affirmation:

As you continue to breathe deeply and rhythmically, repeat the affirmation silently to yourself: "I am worth the effort."

Feel the truth and power behind these words as you repeat them. Imagine them resonating within you.

Body Scan:

Bring your attention to your body. Start at the top of your head and slowly scan down to your toes.

As you focus on each area, repeat the affirmation: "I am worth the effort." Allow any tension or negative thoughts to dissolve as you do this.

Breath Awareness:

Shift your focus to your breath. Observe the natural flow of your breath without trying to control it. With each inhalation, think, "I am." With each exhalation, think, "worth the effort." Feel your worthiness filling you with each breath.

Visualization:

Imagine a radiant light at the core of your being. This light represents your self-worth and self-compassion.

With each breath, visualize this light expanding, filling your entire body with a warm, loving glow. Know that you are worthy of love, care, and effort.

Positive Reflection:

Take a moment to reflect on your accomplishments, both big and small. Recognize the effort you've put into various aspects of your life.

Feel a sense of pride and self-worth as you acknowledge these achievements.

Gratitude:

Shift your focus to the things you appreciate about yourself and your life. Consider the qualities that make you unique and special.

Express gratitude for these qualities and affirm, "I am worth the effort."

Closing:

Take a few more deep breaths, gradually bringing your awareness back to the present moment. When you're ready, open your eyes if they were closed.

This meditation practice can be a powerful tool for boosting your self-worth and self-esteem. Practice it regularly to reinforce the belief that you are indeed worth the effort and love you give to yourself and deserve from others.

SPEAK OUT

JODI PUGH

Jodi Pugh is an open person who tries to be compassionate to all those around her. Over two decades ago, after being sexually abused leading to complex childhood trauma, she spent three years hospitalized in Canada's mental health system. Since then, she has been writing about her experiences and advocating for those who have experienced similar institutionalization.

Jodi lives in Nova Scotia, Canada where she manages her own house cleaning business. She lives with her husband and fur babies.

STARTING OVER ... AGAIN
By
Jodi Pugh

Abuse and neglect negate love. Care and affirmation, the opposite of abuse and humiliation, are the foundation of love. No one can rightfully claim to be loving when behaving abusively.

—bell hooks

Hopeless. That is what I felt in 2021. The same hopelessness I felt while in the hospital over two decades before when I was institutionalized and overweight as a result of being overmedicated. I was on nineteen different medications and felt so much worse than when I'd first entered the hospital. All I wanted then and now was to gain some sense of freedom. It all came tumbling through during COVID, these memories, these feelings, coupled with a deep sense of rejection and abandonment.

Part of my troubles started after a fight I got into. I was in grade nine. This girl was a known fighter. She walked past me and a few of my friends in the school's main hallway on a difficult morning, along with her sister and group of followers. I was feeling out of sorts and irritable. Her sister—let's call her Maggie—said something. I can't recall what it was, although I know whatever she said, it was not said out of love.

As she walked by, I said, "oh fuck off."

Maggie barked, "What did you say!?" and came at me with arms flaring.

"I said *fuck off.*"

Maggie, her sister the fighter, and their friends then started chasing me around the school. I kept walking away, up one hallway and down the next. I knew she was wanting to fight. I was lost for words. The more she said to me, the more choked up I got, which was just gas to their fire. It added to the group of them mocking me.

I felt completely alone.

The bell rang and the doors along the hallways started closing as most of my peers except for one went into their classrooms. I went outside; I could no longer breathe and needed air. There was already a circle forming. My sister was there. She held my hands behind my back. "Don't fight," she said.

It was never my plan to fight, though after the first punch to my face my sister let go of my hands at the same time I ripped them away from her. I remember having this girl on the ground. I wanted to punch her face, but I couldn't. Instead, I hit the ground beside her face over and over again. I don't remember much after that. I do remember someone coming and kicking me in the face. Then a white car with its tire beside my head. Then I see myself choking this girl. A few friends were trying to pull my hands off her neck yelling, "you're gonna kill her!"

I was in complete shock. I did not know what happened and how it was that I was choking her. Blood was all over my shirt. I thought it was so gross having her blood all over me.

Then realized the blood was mine.

I was going in and out of consciousness. I remember laying on the stretcher and them putting an oxygen mask on me. I remember hands and the neck brace. At the hospital they told me I had a concussion and a broken nose. A friend told me more about the fight just a couple years ago. "You were just swinging back and forth like a rag doll as that girl was kicking you right in the side of the head. Over and over again. I thought you'd died," she said.

Then she said I came to, got up, and starting choking the girl. "Just like Hulk," she said, meaning the green monster who was the star of the TV show, the *Incredible Hulk*.

I now understand a bit about how and why our brains and bodies turn off—go into fight, flight, freeze, or fawn mode—when we are in stressful situations. That protective reaction saved me. Then this other part of me—an adrenaline primal part—took over. It's that part you hear that will give someone the strength to lift a car off someone in dire need. It is that part that brought out the fierce mother-bear strength I needed to stop this girl from killing me.

As amazing and heroic as that may sounds, my reactions left me in terror. In terror of myself. Of my strength and my fierce power. This episode left me feeling rejected and bitter towards my peers and friends.

Fast forward to the following summer, the summer before grade ten. I was dabbling in drugs. More depressed. Looking back now, I know that fight did something to my brain. I know more about concussions, more about built-up trauma. Plus, there was some residue from the street drugs in me, on that day, I'm sure.

On that summer day I was feeling really shitty. I wanted out. I wanted to go so far away from my family. So far away from everyone. I felt fed up and unsafe. Either that day, or the day before, I had expressed how I was feeling to a friend. I also told her that my refuge was the trails.

So I was on the trails not far from my home. I went there a lot. I would stand by the river and throw rocks. I would cry. Being there gave me time to just *be*. No judgements, no need to change to make others comfortable. I looked up ahead of me on the trail and was sure the guy I saw walking towards me was Graham, a friend's boyfriend.

He came to me, acting like he'd come looking for me. I asked him how he got there.

"Two feet and a heartbeat," he said. He showed me his right thumb, indicating that he'd hitchhiked.

"Why are you here?" I asked this as I got this terrible feeling in my gut. Though he was a friend's boyfriend, him and I never hung out. This was unusual.

"I thought you'd need some cheering up." He took out a joint. We both smoked it and chatted. I told him I just wanted to take off. That I didn't want to be here anymore. So many of the kids in our school talked about leaving Ontario and going to British Columbia. It was one of those cool things to do; BC was the furthest away from Ontario you could get in Canada. It had this reputation of being more laid-back and freer. I told him I wanted to go there and, "You know, live there and fuck everything else." Happiness was there. It sure sounded like that, so I desperately wanted part of the happiness thing going on in BC, instead of being inside my brain in Ontario where I felt lost, misunderstood, frustrated, and alone.

"Let's go," he said.

"I can't. I'll get in trouble." I remember vividly saying this with such a deep melancholy. I wanted to escape but felt so young, so trapped. Like a newly emerged butterfly not believing in her wings.

Graham started walking down the trail and told me to follow. We walked down from the trail to a forested area. I remember feeling my heartbeat. I can feel it now as I type. I am thirty-nine as I write this and until a couple years ago, I had lost most memory of the rest of that evening. I had only little vague moments of recollection. No knowing of who it was, though my body sure knew. When I fully tampered off my medication, this as well as many other repressed memories and feeling resurfaced.

The first one to come back was me seeing his face. We were on the ground; I was petrified. I saw something in his eyes that was pure evil.

Then I saw me. I was looking down at myself from way above the trees. What I saw was pure misery. Like hell, perhaps. Like I died while still living. I can feel the grief in my throat as I recall this.

I guess the grief stayed with me. What also stayed was the memory of a lady that lived right near that trail. She once said hi to me. She seemed so kind and caring. She felt safe to my soul.

I fantasized we had tea together and that she rescued me. In my fantasy, she wrapped me in a blanket, covered and cleansed my wounds. She covered me. Tea with her would be closure for this memory perhaps.

Closure.

This fantasy tea was also for the time I was abused as a little girl by my grandfather. It was closure for the time I lay on the ground alone in high school after that fight and for a few other times I was violated. It was for all the times I was alone and desperately needed someone.

The day off that trail probably holds the most grief. I remember feeling a tugging on my backpack. I remember seeing my shorts. This was right before it happened. I remember being on the trail hearing myself running afterwards. I was running so fast I could hear my heart beating out my chest. All these things jump from one to another often in the wrong order.

Around the time of this day on the trails, I had left home. I was staying at a friend's place. My family never came to see me, except my dad who came to say I should come home.

I wanted my sister to come; at age fifteen I couldn't express my vulnerability so clearly. Plus everything was mixed up in my head as I was so messed up by drugs and the abuse. I couldn't fully articulate this need. I wanted away from all the chaos at the house, the chaos inside me, and I also wanted a hug. I wanted to feel LOVE. To feel I was given a damn about. I wanted connection and to feel safe in the world.

When I was at my friends, we laughed. We had fun, but at nights I wanted her mom to hold me. I would have never said this to her or anyone. I think I would have collapsed with grief if I'd actually received this. Don't we all need this comfort and love?

I remember one day being downtown and running into my brother and sister. Both were saying that the police were coming to get me. That seemed so heartless when I think of it now, but they were probably stuck in the middle with their own issues of teenagerhood, their own hurt and panic. Those two would often team up and tease me until I would explode; they loved seeing me lose it. It gave them more reasons to make fun of me. I had a terrible temper, and this got them going, which only, of course, made me explode more into my rage.

The school year started. Grade ten. My depression and out of body experiences progressed. I felt like I was in a movie. I felt so much fear. I didn't care, or so I told myself. I didn't care one bit. But I did. You know when you want someone to just sit and be with you, yet the vulnerability it would take to say this is too much. I couldn't ask. I felt so alone.

I'm not sure what broke it all. The fight before. The feeling unsafe at home. The neglect. The sexual abuse that summer. The sexual abuse before. Probably it all. I remember walking downtown and half of me was out of my body. I felt above myself, not fully intact. It was my soul. I came back to school and was then called down to the office.

My mom was there.

She took me out for ice cream. I didn't remember the last time I sat with my mom, let alone having ice cream with her. I sensed her frustration and tension. I told her how I felt. That I was no longer here. That I was so scared. She made an appointment with the doctor. That was the first time I was medicated. An antidepressant. Not long after that, I went into the hospital.

I felt so lost in there, though a bit relieved. It was the quiet: It was so peaceful. My family started to visit, well mostly my mom. I remember sitting on a bench in the smoking area and my mom asked for one of my smokes. Smoking was a habit she tried to hide from us all though the smell of her jacket and clothes had given that away a long time ago. I looked at her and thought, but did not say, *I don't even know you.*

She was raised in the time when parents were authority figures and that's it. We did laugh, we sat down at dinner; but there was so much disconnect in so many ways. In the hospital, I started getting a connection with her, slowly. First with her then with my father. I craved this my whole life. But that fragile sprout of a connection would be hard to draw on, especially in times of loneliness.

I was in and out and shipped all around to a few different hospitals in different places. Each time I was getting more institutionalized, meaning more used to the experience of being forcibly collected, processed, and sleeping in hospital rooms. One thing I noticed from the start though: these people, my people, the "mentally ill," were vulnerable and raw. I could cry, be heard, and validated. Not with the staff, very seldom with them—it was the patients. We all had something in common . . . a broken heart and souls in need of human connection. We got this through deep, shared feelings and conversations. There was also joy. Whatever it was, it was always deep and real.

What was also there, however, was chaos. We had all grown up with it. I was in an institution at age sixteen, during that time when we are all trying to learn who we are and to develop and form an identity. So I did, but it wasn't a healthy identity as I believed my safe place was *there*, in that type of institution. That I needed to be a certain way to be seen and heard. It was also a safe place away from getting more hurt and abused. It was also a place I could go to when I didn't want to be seen and when things got too much.

I learnt that I could go *there*, to the institution, when I felt lonely, but this came at a price. I also learnt that feelings need medication. I believed that the feeling of "love" was like a punishment—although this fear of being exposed by needing others was formed many moons before all this. In time this created this helpless cycle where I could no longer be my true authentic, powered, outspoken self. If I did, I would be beaten down verbally and physically and then medicated. When I couldn't handle my emotions during the times I got to home for a few days, I would react with a violence as flashbacks entered my psyche which meant my family called the authorities to have me put back in a hospital. Sometimes it felt like I did this on purpose so I could get to my safe place, other times it was from sheer terror. I was deep into being institutionalized by then.

These were my people, my place. We stood up for each other, though the chaos and dynamics became this addiction. I became addicted to that chaos for some type of high, especially when feeling lonely or emotional neglected. I would get some touch, the closest thing to a hug, even if that meant being restrained.

I could scream and let all the frustration out and have it witnessed even though it meant a day or two being restrained or days being locked away. It meant many of the folks there would be upset with me. It also meant losing ME. But I didn't know all this then. I also didn't know how this chaos calmed my nervous system down. I couldn't and didn't have space unless I was in the lock down - the isolation. I liked it. And I hated it. It was a break. It was time away from everyone. The noise. The people. It also caused the worst type of separation anxiety, as I couldn't get out, no matter how many times I hammered my fists and feet against the door, pleading with everything in me to let me out. I was trapped and on my own and completely powerless.

What has helped me

The road to recovery was not what I thought. I thought it would be much shorter. That it would be organized and once done, once "healed," *that was it* and recovery would be done and complete. For those of us who have walked a longer path in the chaos and darkness, the road to wellness can be much longer than we feel we can bear.

I am still, twenty years later, a work in progress. Living without fear and rage and hopelessness becomes easier. Though the trauma never fully goes, we just get more self-aware and our resilience increases; we gain more tools. Life becomes manageable. Yet we aren't the same as we could have been before it all—we cannot go back to the carefree, untampered-with, innocent version of ourselves. And this is the hardest thing to accept. Just like any acceptance of a loss, most often it takes a stage of grief, of active mourning, to move through.

What has helped me the most?

1. Grieving has helped the most. Grieving what I did not receive, what I lost. Grieving what I DID receive. Grieving what I could have had. The innocence.

2. One of my biggest outlets for this is writing. I can express my anger, my disdain, my pain, my hurt to my abusers safely through writing. I write to myself about all that I wished I received and that I didn't get. I can express it all. I wrote and still do write angry letters to my abusers where I tell them:

   - What they did and how wrong it was.
   - How what they did made me feel.
   - How violating and terrible what they did was and is.

3. I have moved anger the most through screaming, sometimes when alone in the forest, sometimes through screaming in my car.

4. I have moved anger by aggressively drumming.

5. If you have found an event that has been triggering and you can't seem to use any of your coping skills, put an ice cube on your wrist or splash your face with cold water.

6. Breathing rhythmically in this way: for four seconds, breathe in. Hold for four seconds. Breathe out for six seconds. It works because usually when we panic, we breathe shallowly. By focusing on our breath, we can slow it down. The extra two seconds

I found helps breathe out pent-up air. A book that helped me with this is by Pete Walker (details below).

7. And I remind myself:
   - "This will pass, as it has every other time."
   - "I am safe now."

   I say this as rub my chest in a circular motion or cross my arms over my chest with one hand under my armpit and the other on my arm, to mimic a hug.

8. I rock myself.

9. Sometimes I will ask myself what I need. Usually, it will be something small like a glass of water, a hug, reassurance, or a break outside or to somewhere else until I can regroup. Anything more complicated is usually our brain's chatter.

10. Reading and learning the most I could on trauma and attachment helped. I invite you to read some of the books that helped me:
    - Pete Walker, *Complex PTSD: From Surviving to Thriving: A Guide and Map for Recovering from Childhood Trauma*. CreateSpace Independent Publishing Platform, 2013.
    - Bessel van der Kolk, MD., *The Body Keeps the Score: Brain, Mind, and Body in the Healing of Trauma*. Penguin Books, 2015.
    - Susan Anderson, *The Abandonment Recovery Workbook: Guidance through the Five Stages of Healing from Abandonment, Heartbreak, and Loss*. New World Library, 2016.
    - Harriet Lerner, *The Dance of Anger: A Woman's Guide to Changing the Patterns of Intimate Relationships*. William Morrow Paperbacks, 2014.

About Recovery

Megan and I giggled as we walked down the hall. It was like we both synched into each other's minds as, at exactly the same time, we started to run. We ran and broke free—out of the hospital and into the world.

The hospital was an institution school-like setting for troubled youth and for those who had mental health struggles. Most of us were there due disorders caused by trauma. I was sixteen or seventeen, as was Megan.

As we flew out of the workout area, the staff accompanied us, chasing us, at first, they were not far behind us. The freedom I experienced as we ran out of those doors was pure excitement. My breath stopped for a moment as the fresh air hit my lungs. We ran off the property and all the way to this coffee shop. We were free after months of being cooped up like prisoners.

It wasn't long after our arrival there that the police found us and we ran again. We were still giggling, like kids being caught by fuming parents, as they chased us. We split off from each other, running with everything we had. A female cop caught up with me; I was trying with all my might to fight her off, to continue our great escape. I surrendered after she scraped down my shin with her big, clonking cop boots.

Going back to the hospital, out of breath, with straw and grass in my hair, all I could think about at the time was—*how exciting was that!!*

I honestly didn't care at the time that I had put these folks out—the officers and the hospital staff. It was thrilling, such a sense of freedom. A short high, I knew full well it would come to an end. It was not the first, nor definitely the last, of my attempts.

I often go there, to that memory, during moments of "wanting out." I get these urges to feel free, without the added "excitement" of being arrested. The freedom is not in the sense of the inability to now go outside whenever I want, but a different kind of freedom.

The freedom I examine is a freedom from punishment, from this inner retaliation of suppressed anger and wrongdoing that was put on me way before any institution, well before I entered any psychiatric ward. Freedom from being ignored, gaslit, abused, or put-down when I speak up or put a boundary in place. Freedom from a parent who turned into an inner critic within my psyche. Freedom from peers, from family, who now add to this internal dialogue. Freedom where I can be me, no matter what. Freedom from any consequence as I gain my power—so I can gain my power.

My voice.

The more I find my voice and this power, the more the internal chatter arises, as if an infestation of put-downs that continue to haunt me from within. There are times in this when the grief of it all hits again. Taking me back, as if I'm back at square one wondering where any progress has gone, only to once again rise to higher realm. A new equilibrium that takes some time to call "home."

It's the in between of what we once knew, like our old life. Our old ways of coping that once made us safe, though now no longer fit into where we are headed, to this unknown place of "recovery."

Who am I now as I drift off away from my old life preserver into the unknown sea? Secretly, I'm waiting to be carried and held by the arms of this love that is stable enough to buoy me as I slowly crumple from all the deaths of myself that I've experienced while still alive.

Not having the proper type of the help I needed made my pain snowball into suicidal ideation and attempts. I had a desperate need for love and connection, a need to be seen and heard. The shame of my behaviours was enough for me to want to end my life. I did not realizing my behaviours were due to my attempts to be safe. The shame of my body responses to sexual abuse was another reason I wanted to end things.

To recover, I continue to try to be understood and to get guidance and reasons for all that has gone so wrong. To know none of this was my fault and is confusing; this stuff is often not talked about nearly enough. I developed a need to help bring more understanding of the aftermath of abuse and all the ways it impacted me.

All this past self-blame ended up turning to fury and frustration which then ended up turning inward to depression. For the longest time, I thought someone was going to save me. I read this somewhere and learned it is so true… *I didn't realize that the person who would save me would, in fact, be me.*

This realization has been pretty devastating to come to and has taken a great deal of time to grieve. After a while, something starts snowballing inside those who have experienced trauma after trauma. It happens when you start to realize it was not your fault and who this blame actually belongs to.

Society, religion, and spirituality ("think positive") can easily push certain healthy emotions away, suppressing what is needed for our healing. I have found anger so helpful in many ways, yet I often feel and hear this unhelpful push to:

"Forgive."

"Don't be so bitter and resentful."

"Move on…that was so long ago.."

Or as Harriet Lerner mentions in her book, *The Dance of Anger*, that we, us females, are bitches. Or that we are PMSing. These ways of dismissing us suggest our normal expressions of anger are not warranted and that this anger about what happened to us is, instead, something to do with us being a hormonal female, not a reaction to real hurt. I don't think we as society, especially us women, have allowed all this legitimate and built-up anger out. For the reasons above and also most of us are uncomfortable with this emotion.

However, the most healing remedy for me is allowing this anger to surface and *be*. Healthy healing happens when this healthy fury and truthful expression is allowed to be let out and witnessed. I have fury and want to be witnessed because of:

- All the wrongs and the times I stopped standing up for myself because I did not know how to do it in a healthy way.

- How all that was done to me impacted me, and in fact, has changed me.
- The times I acted more submissive and not empowered because acting small kept me safe.
- When I was fierce it was scary and, in fact, got me hurt many times.

As we navigate through finding our voice after it's been beaten down either emotionally, mentally, physically, our power is like a pendulum continuously swinging back down and around to a more passive stance, then back to an empowered higher self. With each swing, we are getting more free, while noticing the time to withdraw once again, to grieve and to replenish the soul. It is power that is built with firmness, yet grace. With assertiveness. Through being seen and heard. Through speaking back to this internal chatter. Through believing now that I am now safe to do so.

To me, this is freedom.

Help Her RECOVER

The only real prison is fear,
and the only real freedom is
freedom from fear.

~ *Aung San Suu Kyi*

Help Her
RECOVER

By Amanda Willett

SAFETY Principle 3: "I DESERVE TO BE SAFE," is a fundamental theme in the recovery process from gender-based violence. This principle underscores the undeniable right of survivors to live free from fear, threat, and harm. Many survivors of gender-based violence have endured situations where their safety was compromised, leaving them traumatized and hyper-vigilant. Embracing this principle means recognizing that safety is not just a physical state but an emotional and psychological one as well. It involves seeking environments, relationships, and support systems that prioritize safety and well-being. For survivors, reclaiming their sense of safety is a vital step toward healing and rebuilding trust in them- selves and others. This principle empowers survivors to set boundaries, establish safety plans, and access resources that protect them from further harm. Ultimately, it sends a clear message that everyone, regardless of their past experiences, deserves to live a life where they feel secure, valued, and free from the threat of violence.

Jodi Pugh narrative reflects on her tumultuous experiences, trauma, and path to recovery. The story vividly portrays her struggles with feeling safe, both physically and emotionally, as she faces violence, bullying, abuse, and a sense of abandonment.

Her chapter begins with a recount of an intense fight in her high school that led to a traumatic incident, where Jodi felt utterly alone and vulnerable. Her instinctual reactions during the fight left her in shock and filled with terror about her own strength and capacity for violence. This episode left her bitter and isolated from her peers.

Jodi further describes her experiences during a traumatic encounter in the woods, which added to her feelings of fear and insecurity. The story highlights the profound impact of trauma on her mental and emotional well-being, leading to depression and a sense of not belonging anywhere.

Throughout the chapter, Jodi emphasizes her yearning for safety, love, and connection, which she struggled to find within her family and community. She sought refuge in an institution where she felt a sense of belonging and understood by others who had experienced trauma.

Jodi's narrative underlines the complexity of her healing journey. She shares the coping mechanisms she developed, including writing, expressing anger through various outlets, and seeking solace in nature. She also discusses the importance of grieving for what she didn't receive and how it contributed to her healing process.

The chapter touches upon her experience with the mental health system, which she found broken and insufficient in providing the support and understanding she needed. Despite the challenges, Jodi emphasizes her resilience and determination to save herself.

Jodi's story underscores her constant pursuit of safety, not only in terms of physical safety but also emotional safety. She grapples with the aftermath of traumatic events and seeks refuge in places and activities that make her feel secure. Throughout her recovery, she learns to navigate her emotions, develop coping strategies, and find ways to create a sense of safety for herself.

Jodi's journey highlights the importance of acknowledging and addressing the safety needs of survivors of gender-based violence. It also emphasizes the significant role that understanding, support, and proper mental health care play in the healing process.

Jodi serves as a powerful testament to the resilience of survivors and the critical role of empathy and community support in helping them reclaim their sense of safety and well-being.

SAFETY

Principle 3:
I DESERVE TO BE SAFE

Which emotion(s) am I trying to avoid right now?
Why am I trying to hide from this emotion?
What does this emotion need from me?

Affirmation:

No harm will come my way. There's a higher power keeping me safe. The universe has my back and is protecting me.

Child's Pose

Child's Pose, a resting pose, feels like the ultimate safe-haven. It's calming, encourages strong and steady breathing, and stretches your back, hips, thighs, and shoulders. To get into Child's Pose, you'll start in Tabletop Pose on your mat. Sink your hips to your heels and place your forehead on the floor.

You can opt to stretch your arms out in front of you, place them alongside your body with your palms up, or fold them in front of you while your forehead rests on your palms. Focus on taking full, deep breaths and allowing your body to sink into your mat.

Mindful Focusing Meditation

This practice can be particularly helpful when you're feeling anxious, stressed, or in need of a moment of peace. Find a quiet and comfortable place to sit or lie down, and let's begin:

Posture and Comfort:

Sit or lie down in a comfortable position. Keep your back straight, but not rigid, to allow for relaxed breathing. Place your hands on your lap or gently on your knees. Close your eyes if you're comfortable doing so

Deep Breathing:

Begin by taking a few deep, calming breaths. Inhale slowly through your nose, allowing your abdomen to expand, and exhale slowly through your mouth, releasing any tension. With each breath, imagine that you are letting go of any stress or worries.

Grounding:

Bring your attention to your body and the physical sensations of being supported by the ground or your chair. Feel the weight of your body and the points of contact with the surface beneath you. Visualize roots extending from your body into the earth, anchoring you in a safe and stable foundation.

Affirmation:

Silently repeat a calming affirmation that resonates with you, such as "I am safe" or "I am secure. Let this affirmation be your mantra as you continue to breathe deeply.

Body Scan:

Start at the top of your head and slowly scan down through your body, paying attention to any areas of tension or discomfort. As you identify areas of tension, imagine your breath flowing into those areas, soothing and relaxing them.

Breath Awareness:

Shift your focus to your breath. Observe the natural rhythm of your breath without trying to control it. With each inhalation, imagine a sense of safety and peace filling your body. With each exhalation, release any remaining tension or worry.

Visualization:

Visualize a serene and safe place. It could be a cozy room, a peaceful forest, a tranquil beach, or any location where you feel completely safe. Imagine yourself there, feeling the security and peace that this place provides.

Positive Reflection:

Take a moment to reflect on the aspects of your life that bring you a sense of safety and security. Acknowledge the people, places, and practices that contribute to your well-being.

Gratitude:

Shift your focus to gratitude for the safety you have in your life. Express thanks for the feeling of security, the people who support you, and the circumstances that provide you with safety.

Closing:

Take a few more deep breaths, gradually bringing your awareness back to the present moment. When you're ready, open your eyes if they were closed. This meditation practice can help you reconnect with a sense of safety and calmness. Regular practice can strengthen your feelings of security and provide you with a reliable tool for finding peace in challenging moments.

SPEAK OUT

MARTHA MILLS

Martha is a certified yoga therapist also trained in violence prevention and intervention. She is passionate about teaching a whole-bodied approach to healing. During her studies, Martha focused on bringing land-based healing techniques and ceremonies into sexual trauma recovery.

Martha's training includes an 800 hr IAYT certification in Yoga Therapy. She teaches Pranayama and respiratory health classes, and Restorative yoga classes all through a trauma-informed lens and sees clients on a 1-1 basis focusing on nature-based healing, soul retrieval, and somatic movement. She is also a lead trainer in TRMBW & SEL at Rituals for Recovery.

Born in the UK, she now resides in Vancouver, BC, Canada.

UNFREEZING
By
Martha Mills

If you put shame in a petri dish, it needs three ingredients to grow exponentially: secrecy, silence, and judgement. If you put the same amount of shame in the petri dish and douse it with empathy, it can't survive.

—Brene Brown

This is the story of the unfreezing, the returning to myself.

I was there curled up, my knees held tightly into my body, my head hung down to my chest, feeling totally cold, numb, and deeply afraid. My body was shaking with fear, fear of not being believed, fear of not knowing how to get out the words that were stuck in my throat and pounding in my chest. How do I explain?

My attention returned to my manager. I was sitting in the passenger seat of his warm car. He was looking at me, repeatedly asking what was wrong. There was deep concern in his voice. "Should I take you to the police station? Did you need to go to the hospital? What do you need?"

I could not speak. Tears rolled down my cheeks as I struggled to figure out how to answer him. I knew I couldn't make myself small enough. I wanted to disappear; I didn't know how to articulate the experience. I could not understand then that it would take months.

I was in Canada, the first place I'd spent much time. Partly because of the pandemic, I'd been there nearly four years ago after ten years of traveling the world working on boats/yachts as a deckhand, tour-guiding, working in hostels, adventure tourism and teaching yoga. I had no real home in England to return to, and being on the road became my home, meeting new people and having new experiences.

I moved fluidly, like the rivers and oceans I loved. At times life was turbulent, scary, and rough, but there were also so many moments of beauty and calm where I felt like I was the luckiest person in the world. Although, of course, being a solo traveler and working in a predominantly male industry, there were always moments of uncertainty. Still, even in situations when I was tested, I always made it out unscathed; however, this time, I was not so lucky.

The Worst 24 Hours of My Life

It felt like it happened very quickly. I awoke to a man's weight on me. He was rubbing rough and calloused hands all over my body. His breathing was heavy, and he was groaning in my ear. Like he was enjoying himself, and me telling him, yelling at him, to get off me meant nothing to him. He didn't go as I said, stop over and over again. It was like he couldn't hear me or more; what I said didn't matter. I fought him off as he whispered that he would make me not feel lonely anymore - something I had brought up when everyone was sitting around talking at the hostel. Him using my own words as a reason for why he was doing what he was doing to me.

The smell of cigarette smoke made me gag as he moved his hands to my face. I was trapped in the bottom bunk, feeling closed in, my fists pounding on him, wondering how to get to the door, seeing the slats of the top bunk as I was there squished against the wall, terrified, doing all I could to move his heavy weight off of me. Then I was suddenly free.

I scrambled off the floor and fled to the bathroom, where I locked the door. I held onto the sink for support, shaking, feeling like I was going to throw up, and tears streaming down my face and shaking.

I was alone in the hostel when I dared to leave the bathroom. He had fled. I stayed awake, bags ready, waiting for my boss to arrive so I could get away.

I heard my boss make a call to the police, the infamous Mounties of the Royal Canadian Mounted Police (RCMP). He was saying he had someone in his car who had been assaulted. I felt so small, damaged, and broken, my knees wrapped up under my chin, trying to understand why I felt so jarred. I could not comprehend anything—had I said those words to my boss? Has "an assault" really happened? He was now driving to the police station.

Arriving at the RCMP, the female officer I spoke to was friendly and caring but wanted more details than I could remember. I could hear the questions being asked, she needed to know what had happened, but I had no way to respond. The voice that came out of my mouth was not mine. The story it was telling did not feel real. I felt like I was in the middle of a terrible dream and that I would wake up soon, but it was no dream. Yet it did not feel real. Like my boss, the police officer asked if I needed to go to the hospital. Then she told me I had to go to get a swab done.

But I would not. I didn't want anyone to touch me or go near me. At that moment, I thought—but I'm unsure if I said this aloud—that there was no point in a swab. I had gotten him off me before he fully penetrated me with his penis, and all I was thinking was that no one would believe me. The point of the swab was "evidence. Who would believe me without evidence? Is DNA of hands evidence?

Frozen

The idea of pressing charges weighed heavily on me. Part of me knew that I should and needed to, but I was scared because it didn't feel real. Did it count as assault? He had not fully penetrated me. There was no evidence.

Soon I left my boss's home to return to the tent in the forest I had been living in where I was working for the summer as a zipline guide. I felt comfortable being away from people. No one could harm me there. I had the peace and the loving embrace of Mother Nature, and it felt comforting to be away from people where I could sit with my emotions. I needed to be away from the questions I could not answer and the expectation that I should 'do' something. Even with the peace during those days, I was dazed. I returned to work because I didn't know what else to do; I wanted to believe nothing had happened. I honestly thought that making myself busy with work and pretending it didn't happen would make the experience disappear. So, for six days a week, I worked as an outdoor adventure guide, acting enthusiastic and extrovert for long hours, pushing and exhausting myself so that maybe I would be so tired that I would sleep. I felt the safety of mother nature back home in my tent, but it still wasn't enough on its own to soothe me.

For those two months, I did not sleep. I tried. I tried to sleep every night, but my body was rigid, ready to fight off another attack. Even though my mind knew I was somewhere safe, the message wasn't getting through to my body. My body was doing what it thought was the best thing to keep me safe and that was keeping me on high alert but this involuntary reaction was more harmful than good.

The nights were long, and the days were longer. I was so dazed from lack of sleep, and my body was stiff and tense from being on guard 24/7, waiting for something terrible to happen. I kept thinking he was going to turn up at my work. Anyone with the same beard and body shape caused me to panic and my breath to become short.

Some days it felt like everyone was expecting me to be ok, and I asked myself why the assault still affected me. I started to get panic attacks and found it hard to breathe. Every time I smelt cigarette smoke, I would have a powerful physical reaction in my body, and it would take me back to the incident, being trapped again and fighting to escape. A strong, rigid feeling in my body. How I longed to flow again.

I was scared to breathe into my body, to feel myself within it. I knew if I did, then I would be reminded of his rough, tobacco-smelling hands pulling at my body. I didn't want to feel his beer breath on my skin. I didn't want to acknowledge the struggle that my muscles and physical body had been through trying to get away, to get out from underneath him as his weight held me captive against the wall. He was between me and the safety that was beyond the door. I didn't want to have to be reminded of his grunting and groaning.

Throughout that summer, the RCMP kept contacting me, saying that I had to decide whether I was going to press charges. I felt cornered and trapped as I didn't know what to say, overwhelmed by the responsibility of making this decision. It felt like a lonely and personal decision that no one could help me navigate, so I ignored their calls.

I decided to leave the forest and work in the fall and I went back to Vancouver, and that's where I realized I'd have to make a change, as I couldn't continue to live with these feelings of fear and despair anymore. Not that I had a plan. I just needed more recognition and support for all that I felt, and it felt hard to find that, especially during a pandemic.

I was relieved to find a therapist, I managed to find a therapist who had just graduated and could see me on a grandfather scale which meant I paid $30 otherwise I would never have been able to afford this help. It brought a tsunami of relief. Finally, I found someone who wanted to help me, believed me, and together we slowly started to repair the damage.

Body in Shut-Down

Back in Vancouver, my body finally collapsed, and I became still. It happened when I tried to get a part-time job to distract myself once again. I was worried about money and how I could afford to live; I just wanted to be and feel normal again. Two weeks into this new job, I had a panic attack while at work I froze and broke down. My body forced me to stop and rest, she needed healing, attention, and love, and I had to face and come to terms with what I had been through. For a few months after that, I couldn't work. I could only socialize with a few close people for a few hours, I didn't go out anywhere at night, I saw my therapist at least once a week. It would be a long journey to feel freer and unfreeze, feel myself within my body, and flow again. But I was now on my way.

Sitting on my bedroom floor, I decided to google the definition of sexual assault. It was now three months after the attack. It was then that I realized what had happened. I couldn't deny it anymore. At that point, I had been working with my counselor weekly, but even with her, the story and the words coming out of my mouth did not feel like mine. But now it took that moment to accept, to know, that I had been sexually assaulted and that however much I tried to avoid it, the assault was now part of my life story. It was woven into the tapestry of my journey through life. There was nothing I could do about that fact and its power to change the trajectory of my life.

I felt so much shame and guilt around what had happened some days it was almost unbearable. I felt that my body, the way I looked, and the person I was had caused me to be attacked and that I had done this to myself. It was an overwhelming and heavy feeling to be carrying around. I stopped making eye contact. I didn't want anyone to know the undeserving person that I was. I felt like less of a person and that I didn't deserve to be respected.

Living Becomes an Out-of-Body Experience

During the first year after the assault, I would dissociate often. I would suddenly feel terrified and overwhelmed with fear that I would just have to put myself to bed and put a pillow on my back as, for some reason, I knew that if I protected my back, then I was safe. I would hold onto my foot as I lay there so that at least I would feel a little present in my body. After that, I would just wait to feel better.

Showering and being able to look at my body in the mirror was hard for me to do. I felt I didn't even recognize the body I was looking at. It felt like an unknown place to be now. I would feel scared by how overwhelming that felt, and that overwhelming feeling would always lead to thoughts about how much I didn't want to be here and that it had already felt like I had disappeared. This is how my dissociation showed up for me.

I remember needing new clothes, but I was too afraid to go shopping, and when I tried to shop online, I became scared. The models looked too promiscuous to me, and I was fearful for their safety. I didn't want the clothes they were wearing as I didn't want to draw attention to myself. I don't want to invite what happened to happen again.

Yoga had always been something in my life that had kept me present in my body and had given me such joy, but with this feeling that my body had betrayed me, my body was an unsafe place to be. I found that I was scared to try a practice I used to love, I then discovered trauma-informed yoga, and I studied a course online where I would learn how to teach this style. It was hard going, I still had flashbacks often while practicing, but it was the perfect place to start communicating with my body and practicing and learning nervous system regulation. I had an inkling that returning to yoga would help me feel safe enough to begin to move my body again. It would be a crucial part of my unfreezing.

Learning to Be Me

It took a lot of work to get to where I am today, and it wasn't easy. And I'm not finished with the healing .

I had to relearn how to be me again. And that has been messy and confusing. For a long time, I believed I was assaulted because I deserved it, that I was somehow not worthy of being treated with respect, and that my body was nothing.

I needed to understand more about everything that my body and I were experiencing, and I threw myself into gaining as much knowledge as possible so that I could help myself and one day help others not experience all that I was going through. After learning about trauma-informed yoga, I went back to school to study yoga therapy. During these two years I learned so much about nervous system health, neuroscience, restorative therapeutics, and the PolyVagal theory, which has been a massive factor in helping me connect and understand how to move through this experience.

Volunteering on a crisis line in Vancouver also helped me to feel that I wasn't alone in my experience, every day I would get calls from the bravest women who also had not given up and knew they would be strong again, being on the crisis line and listening to the callers' stories humbled me and helped me heal in ways I didn't know I would. To feel a connection and just to be there to support women who were feeling the same as me was so powerful. It gave me the purpose not to disappear.

The last three years have been the most challenging years of my life. To feel that level of unsafety in my own body was terrifying, but through all this self-learning, school, and connection with other women, I now know that my body reacted in the most caring and protective way that it knew how to. I now know I am not broken or flawed because of this experience and how he made my body feel. I know that I deserve love and to be in a loving relationship with someone, that I am deserving of good things despite how he made me feel. It continues to be challenging, but I know that I fight to keep going every day, and healing means that I won. And he didn't.

Returning to Nature

I now live with my partner in a small mountain town in British Columbia. I have become a registered Yoga therapist working with individuals who have experienced trauma. I use ceremony and land-based healing techniques to help survivors feel safe again in their bodies and connect with the world around them. Nature teaches us many lessons about resilience, interconnectedness, healing, and restoration. And I learned that firsthand from the safety of my tent in my forest home that summer of 2020 to returning to Vancouver and just having to learn to be present on the days when all I had the courage to do was to walk around the block, I would see flowers blooming in between cracks in the pavement and it would remind me to stay strong and to keep going.

This experience made me more attuned with my body in a way I didn't know was possible. I know how to create safety for myself and regulate my nervous system and understand myself better. I know the importance of reaching out for help and the power of standing up and saying; please help me. How important it is to witness our healing, whether by a professional or Mother Nature herself. Although I don't travel as much anymore, I have found the richness in stillness and the simplicity in the fact that I am here. And I am safe.

Help Her RECOVER

Just breathe. You are strong enough to handle your challenges, wise enough to find solutions to your problems, and capable enough to do whatever needs to be done.

~ Lori Deschene

Help Her RECOVER

By Amanda Willett

BREATH Principle 4: "MY BREATH IS MY MOST POWERFUL TOOL" emphasizes the significance of self-care, mindfulness, and resilience in the journey of recovery from gender-based violence. Survivors often experience emotional and psychological wounds that affect their mental well-being. This principle encourages survivors to recognize the healing power of their breath and the importance of self-awareness. Through practices like meditation, deep breathing exercises, and mindfulness, survivors can regain a sense of control over their emotions and reactions. It reminds them that, even in the face of adversity, their breath remains a constant source of strength and resilience. This principle underscores the idea that survivors can harness their inner resources to find calm, stability, and healing, allowing them to move forward on their path to recovery with a greater sense of empowerment and self-awareness.

Martha Mills, shares her personal journey of healing after experiencing sexual assault. highlighting the profound impact that trauma can have on one's physical and emotional well- being, particularly in relation to the breath.

Martha describes her initial response to the assault, which left her feeling frozen and unable to speak about her experience. Her body's response to the trauma, characterized by fear, panic, and dissociation, prevented her from using her breath effectively. She struggled to articulate what had happened and was overwhelmed by shame and guilt, leading her to isolate herself and disconnect from her own body.

The theme of breath becomes evident in Martha's journey towards healing. She recounts how she gradually learned to reconnect with her body through trauma-informed yoga and other therapeutic practices. These practices helped her regulate her nervous system and regain a sense of safety within herself. Martha's description of using her breath as a tool for nervous system regulation highlights its importance in the healing process.

Over time, Martha's journey led her to seek professional help and connect with other survivors, both of which played pivotal roles in her recovery. She realized that her body's reactions to the trauma were not signs of weakness but rather protective mechanisms. Through her experiences, she learned to be present in her body again and to appreciate the value of self-care and self-compassion. In the end, Martha's story illustrates how trauma can disrupt the natural flow of breath and the importance of finding ways to restore that connection. By embracing healing practices, seeking support, and recognizing the significance of her own breath, she found a path toward recovery and self-empowerment.

BREATH

Principle 4:
MY BREATH IS MY MOST POWERFUL TOOL

What emotions or situations tend to disrupt
my natural breathing patterns?

How can I use my breath to regain control in those moments?

Affirmation:

My breath is a bridge to inner peace and a source of resilience.

Yoga Pose: Warrior 2, Virabhadrasana II

If you want to feel strong, steady, and focused, Warrior II is just the pose to practice. Start in a High Lunge with your right leg forward, then open your hips to face the left and bring your back foot parallel to the back edge of the mat. Sink deeper into your legs while you align your spine vertically and extend your arms out horizontally. Reach out through your fingers and bring your gaze forward. Switch sides.

Mindful Mantra Meditation:

This practice can help you connect with your breath, find inner peace, and build resilience. Find a quiet and comfortable place to sit or lie down before you begin:

Get Comfortable: Sit or lie down in a comfortable position. You can use a cushion or chair for added comfort. Rest your hands gently on your lap or by your sides.

Straighten Your Posture: Maintain an upright but relaxed posture. Close your eyes if you're comfortable doing so. If not, you can keep them softly focused on a spot in front of you.

Become Aware of Your Breath: Begin by taking a few deep breaths. Inhale slowly through your nose, allowing your lungs to fill completely. Exhale gently through your mouth, letting go of any tension.

Natural Breathing: Allow your breath to return to its natural rhythm. Notice the sensation of your breath as it enters and leaves your nostrils or the rise and fall of your chest or abdomen.

Focus on the Breath: Pay full attention to your breath. As you inhale, silently say to yourself, "I am inhaling." As you exhale, say, "I am exhaling." Continue this pattern, using your breath as a bridge to stay present in the moment.

Observe Without Judgment: Thoughts and distractions may arise. When they do, simply acknowledge them without judgment. Imagine placing each thought on a leaf and letting it float away down a peaceful stream, bringing your attention back to your breath.

Feel the Resilience: As you continue to focus on your breath, feel the sense of resilience growing within you. Each breath you take nourishes your inner strength and peace. Visualize this resilience as a warm, glowing light spreading through your entire body.

Silent Affirmations: As you breathe in, silently affirm, "I am strong." As you exhale, affirm, "I am at peace." Repeating these affirmations with each breath reinforces your inner strength and calm.

Expand Your Awareness: Gradually expand your awareness beyond your breath to your entire body. Feel the sensations in your body, any areas of tension, or relaxation. Allow your breath to continue anchoring you in this state of presence.

Closing: When you're ready to conclude, take a few deeper breaths. Gently wiggle your fingers and toes. Slowly open your eyes if they were closed. Carry this sense of inner peace and resilience with you into the rest of your day.

This mindfulness meditation practice can help you cultivate a deeper connection with your breath, which serves as a bridge to inner peace and resilience. Regularly practicing this meditation can enhance your ability to stay centered, calm, and resilient in the face of life's challenges.

SPEAK OUT

ANGELA BALTKOIS

Angela Baltkois is an entrepreneur who has founded three award-winning businesses during her lifetime. Angela has had the benefit of working with thousands of small, medium and enterprise level businesses, and has coached start up and established businesses in nearly every business sector. A true philanthropist at heart, Angela has volunteered her time and expertise to many charities and non-profits for the past twenty-five years.

Angela Baltkois is a mother of four daughters and grandmother of five. After several abusive relationships she healed herself and found her perfect soulmate. Angela is a strong advocate for equality and social justice. She resides in Cobourg, Ontario with her husband, rescue cats and teenage daughters.

THE TRUTH
By
Angela Baltkois

Never forget that walking away from something unhealthy is brave even if you stumble a little on your way out the door.

—Mandy Hale

In September 1985, I flew from my home in Edmonton, Canada to meet my biological father in Northern England. I was seventeen and my parents separated when I was six months old. My father had been living in Canada at the time but went back to England and never returned. We had no contact at all up until a year before he sent me the tickets to visit him in England. During the trip, I told him how difficult it was dealing with my abusive teenage boyfriend, Doug, back home on my own. He was shocked when I explained that I had actually been in the foster care system since I was twelve and had only recently been released by the system and set up to live on my own. My biological mom still lived with her husband who had abused me three thousand kilometers away from my Edmonton home. in London, Ontario.

So, at age seventeen, I managed to break up with Doug and get my own apartment, but Doug found out where I lived and refused to leave me alone. He would gain entrance to the building and bang on my door, begging me to let him inside. He'd do this until neighbors called the police and the police would arrive and threaten to charge BOTH of us for disturbing the peace. Then one morning I opened the curtains to my ground floor apartment and found him sleeping on the patio. I was afraid he would never stop trying to weasel his way back into my life.

My dad was rightfully worried. "Stay with us," he said, and then he did everything he could to convince me to stay with him and his sweet, welcoming wife and their three young children. He even introduced me to Robert, his car mechanic, and set me up on a date with him. The date went well, and my dad included him in practically every activity we did during my visit. When it was time for me to fly back home, I decided to stay. When I didn't return home on the date I was supposed to, Doug somehow found my dad's phone number and bombed his phone, sending him non-stop, abusive, threatening phone calls. My Dad reinforced that staying in the UK was the right decision and that was it.

I was excited to start a new life with my newfound dad and his young family. I went to school and started looking for a part-time job. A few weeks later, Dad went out for a beer with Robert, and the two of them decided that it would be best if I moved in with Robert instead of staying with my dad.

I was stunned, as no doubt you are reading this story. I was a child in a new continent far from home. This unexpected situation left me disappointed, confused, and sad, plus I could not see a way out of it. I was not ready to move in with Robert. He was ten years older than me and going through a messy divorce (his wife had left him for his best friend). We had just started dating; I knew very little about him. Years later my father told me that it was his sweet wife who "forced" him to do that. Having me around upset her because she told him, "your daughter is so beautiful—she must make you think of her mother all the time." Her real problem with me was that I represented her husband's past. As a woman, I understood.

My dad and stepmother set me up in my own room at Robert's house. Of course, that imagined chaste situation didn't last long; Robert was in my bedroom every night, or I in his. A few months later, I was pregnant. But even though the pregnancy was unplanned, I was ecstatic. I was so excited about the new life growing inside me. I gave birth to our beautiful little daughter Chrystal a couple of months after my eighteenth birthday, and then married Robert the same year on Christmas Eve. We bought a cozy two-bedroom semi-detached home on South Beach Estate in Blyth, Northumberland England just a short distance away from the North Sea. I had plenty of friends my own age who also had babies and mortgages.

When I was twenty-one, we moved to London, Ontario—close to where my mother and the rest of my family resided. The years passed and we had what I thought was a pretty good marriage. We moved often; we were rarely in the same place for two years. Robert would fight with our neighbors, plus he always wanted a bigger and better home. Money was always really tight, yet Robert was adamant that I not work outside the home. Instead, I found ways to help by selling Avon and babysitting other children. I realize now how controlling Robert was back then, but it seemed a good life. For example, not only did he not want me to work outside the home, he also preferred that I didn't leave home at all. When I did go out shopping or to visit friends, he would compare where I said I went with readings of the car odometer. He did not like me to visit my mom without him there, partly because he had a strange jealousy of any time that I spent with my younger brothers who still lived at home. In order to see them, I would tell him I was going shopping and sneak in a visit. As mostly, I was compliant, Robert and I got along fine.

Things started to change after our second daughter, Kelsey, was born. I found I liked working and bringing more money into the family. A new financial opportunity in a network marketing company required me to do evening meetings with my business partners. Robert and I were balancing things fairly well until this time. But now, he did everything he could to try to stop me from going to the meetings.

One evening I had an event booked at my mother's home. But just as I was ready to go, I discovered Robert had left with our family vehicle. I found a babysitter to watch the kids and got a ride from a friend to the meeting. When I got home, I invited my friend in for tea. She asked me if she could borrow something, so I went into the basement to get it for her. By the time I retrieved it, Robert was sitting in a chair in the dark at the bottom of the basement stairs. He ran upstairs ahead of me, and blocked the door from the outside so I couldn't get out of the basement. He was *very* angry because I found a way to get to the meeting even though he took our car.

My friend was not afraid of him. She yelled at him to let me out of the basement. When he refused, she called the police. That was the first of many calls to the police. Robert's aggressive behavior escalated to even scarier levels. At one point he picked up a heavy, thirty-inch tube TV and threw it in my direction - in front of my oldest daughter, Chrystal. He made "jokes" about me that only he thought was funny. For instance, we were renovating our home and he told my mother that he was going to murder me and stuff my body in the walls of our basement. He got into details about how he would do it and not get caught. She was terrified for me and it really shook her up—especially as she told me it sounded researched and planned out. He'd claimed he would cover me with a vapor barrier that would even hide the smell of decomposition.

For a year, as our fights got more and more serious in terms of their level of violence, he would leave me and our kids for days at a time. Finally, he left saying that he didn't love me and was in a relationship with my best friend. The truth is, I knew about his relationship with my friend, but I'd hoped he would end it and we could fix our marriage.

I was completely devastated and the thought of being a single mom and alone for the rest of my life scared me. After the terrible childhood I had due to an abusive stepfather, there was no way that I was going to subject my children to having a stepfather. Or so I thought. The weekend my husband moved out; I met Joseph. He was nice to me and that is all it took. I felt grateful that another man could be attracted to me as Robert repeatedly said I was not pretty and that my body was ruined from carrying babies.

Robert had chosen to move out yet he would not leave me alone. He stalked and harassed me, threatening to burn the house down with me and our children in it. He would call to tell me the license plates of every car that was on my driveway and describe in detail how he was going to kill me. One night, I got up in the middle of the night to use the washroom and I saw him standing in the backyard watching the house. That night he damaged the pool pump so the swimming pool could not be used. I was very afraid and believed that he was going to harm me. I reported many incidents to the police but said there was nothing they could do as I had no proof—they said it was "my word against his."

My youngest, teenage brother decided to help. He stayed at my house and slept on the couch with a baseball bat—ready to defend us if Robert showed up. Eventually I managed to get a restraining order against him, but the court ordered that I still had to meet Robert so he could visit his daughters. He terrorized me and whoever came with me whenever we met for the exchange for his scheduled visits. Usually, I brought my mother or my brother but on one occasion, I brought my new boyfriend, Joseph. He insisted on it, thinking it would get my ex-husband to back off if he saw I had someone willing to protect me.

Joseph respectfully stayed in the car, but my ex came to my side of the car saying horrible things to me. When he called me a c***Joseph got out of the car saying "you are not going to talk to her like that." He yelled at Robert, telling him to leave me alone, "or else." Things escalated and they got into a bloody fist fight in a busy shopping mall parking lot. It was a horrific and devastating thing to watch. I didn't want to see either one of them get hurt. After that incident I took the advice from my friends and family and moved to a different city that was three hours away.

The stalking and harassment continued for several years. Sadly, he used our children as weapons against me. So many horrible things happened during that period of our breakup and the following years that I could write an entire book on that alone. Eventually, I got the proof the police needed. Robert was charged after leaving a message on my answering machine saying that he was going to break every bone in my back.

Unfortunately, I did not have a happy ever after with my new love. Joseph swept me off my feet and helped me get through those dark days after my marriage breakup. He told me that I was beautiful and made me feel worthy of love. We got married, but our marriage only lasted a few years because he refused to hold a steady job. The constant financial uncertainty ruined our marriage. Looking at the bright side, it did force me to work hard and push even harder with my business so that I could make enough money to support our family. By the time we split up, I had grown my business to having two full-time staff and an office outside of my home. I had become a strong, successful businesswoman. I ended our marriage because I knew that I deserved better. And I knew that I could look after my family on my own.

Not long after I split up with husband number two, I met my worst nightmare. Let's call him Phil. He was a charming and very funny man who I met during a business course we both attended. We started hanging out, and although I was not attracted to him at first, I felt that I should give him a chance as he seemed different in a way to the men I usually dated and married. He was funny, spontaneous, intelligent, and very generous. He owned his own home and had a good job—so different from my second ex-husband who was still jobless at that point and had moved back into his parents' basement, which is where he lived when I first met him.

I enjoyed spending time with Phil. My eldest daughter, Chrystal, had left and moved in with her father, Robert, so it was just me and my now thirteen-year-old, Kelsey; she also adored him. We seemed to have so much in common and he was fun! After dating for only a few months, Phil started showing me houses in the country that he thought would be perfect for us. We talked about our future a lot. At the time I was surprised that he wanted to move in together so quickly. I suggested that we could live at my house and rent his house out to "test the water." He was not open to that at all and continued to drive by houses for sale to show them to me until he finally convinced me to look at one. It was a rustic Viceroy in the beautiful forests of northern Ontario, hundreds miles from where my home and friends and family were. We talked about renovating it and filling it with children.

After just nine months of being together, we sold both of our houses and purchased that country house. I was blissfully happy. My daughter was happy. I thought that we would live happily ever after. But within weeks of moving into our new home, Phil went from being a fun-loving guy into an extremely angry and controlling monster. He would come inside the house after work and freak out if we forgot to turn a light off in a room. He put a lock on the door of his office and refused to give me a key or allow me to access it. This was not the same man who had given me a key to his previous house and had allowed my daughter and I to be there when he wasn't there! He refused to contribute money towards the necessary repairs and renovations we both agreed to do to the house. I had dumped all of the equity from my house into our new home. He also had equity from his house and this was supposed to be used on the necessary repairs and renovations our new house needed. Instead, he withheld it.

Then Phil decided that he should only pay one third of the mortgage and household bills because my daughter Kelsey was also living there. He quit his job because he felt that I needed his help to run my company. By that point I had grown the business to employ three full-time staff and several part-time contractors. He quit his job to help me manage the staff even though I repeatedly told him I didn't want him to do that. Even his family tried to talk him out of quitting his job—he wouldn't listen.

Phil proceeded to take over and control every single aspect of my life. He hated all of my friends; therefore, I was not allowed to hang out with them. He undermined my business decisions which confused my staff and wound up making them feel that he was in charge, and I was not. He made a point of embarrassing me in front of my staff, his friends, and both of our families. He loved throwing parties, and his friends would tell me how lucky I was to have him—but they had no idea of the instability he was creating behind our closed doors. He regularly beat our two cats because they went on his couch in the living room. They weren't even *allowed* in the living room and if he thought he heard them, in the middle of the night, he would jump out of bed and run to the living room to catch them in the act just so he could beat them with his slippers. Phil decided that Kelsey's grades were not good enough and that she needed to spend an hour every day writing study notes in addition to her regular homework. And if she was away for a night or at her Dad's house for the weekend, she was forced to make up for hours missed because she was away. He was critical of everything she did and would force her to redo her chores saying they weren't done well enough. If I said anything, a huge fight would occur. I felt as though I had no control over anything at all in my life—even my own daughter. My daughter and I walked on eggshells to try to keep the peace and prevent this man from getting angry. He was terrifying when he was angry because he would get really close to my face, yelling and waving his arms. I was sure that he was going to hit me.

He had road rage like I have never seen before. If someone cut him off in traffic, he would follow them to their destination and when they left their car, he would scratch their car or spit on it. When he was angry at me or other drivers on the road, he would drive fast and erratically. It was terrifying. *He* was terrifying and *so* very mean to my daughter and our cats. To this day it still scares me to think of how much he changed and how quickly he went from that fun-loving man I dated to the frightening bully he became.

There were several occasions when I was so close to leaving him; I was ready to go stay at a women's shelter. The only reason I didn't was I was running my business out of the basement of our home. I had staff that came to work there every day. After less than a year of living together, I sat him down to talk about our living arrangements. I suggested that we should get counseling.

He was firmly against it. He said that I needed counseling and that our troubles were my fault. He said I made him behave the way he did. He told me that he would take the house and my business if we split up. One evening he came into my office and sat in a chair barricading the door; he berated me for hours, telling me that I was crazy. He even brought up things that happened to me as a child, things I'd told him in confidence— he said even *those* things that happened to me as a child were my fault.

He was positioned in front of the door, so I was trapped and unable to remove myself from the horrific things he was saying to me. He challenged me to call the police, so I did. He grabbed the phone from me and hung it up, but I must have been on the 911 call long enough for the police to find our location. They arrived and forced him to leave. The officers expressed concern when I showed them some of the emails he had written to me and when I told them that he regularly beat our cats. Despite their advice, I refused to press charges against Phil. They convinced me to seek help and emphasized that I should not allow him back into the home.

The weeks following his departure were devastating for me. I cried more tears than I have ever cried. I was sad for the loss of the future I thought I had with him. I thought it was entirely my fault for making him behave the way that he did. Three months after he left, I was shocked to discover I was pregnant. Imagine: I was a thirty-eight-year-old single mom of a fourteen- and a nineteen-year-old. I was isolated, living in the country, away from supportive friends. My family was over a three hours' drive away.

When I told Phil that I was expecting, he harassed me non-stop for weeks, ordering me to have an abortion. But I couldn't. That was never an option for me. He finally went away, then re-appeared a couple of weeks before my baby was born. He managed to convince me to allow him to move back into the spare bedroom so I would have someone to drive me to the hospital when I went into labor. He agreed that he would stay only temporarily and only for as long as I needed his help. So, I let him come back. Immediately he fought to control everything again and I realized my mistake.

He would not allow my daughter to come to the hospital with me when I was in labor and once the baby was born and we were back at home, he decided she had a cold and would not let her near her new little sister. He forced me to name our child with the name and middle names he wanted and demanded to go to the registry office with me to make sure I did it.

He hated that I was breastfeeding and insisted that our daughter needed to be bottle fed. He would hold my crying baby, refusing to give her to me so I could feed her. He would yell at me while holding my crying newborn in his arms. He was meaner than ever to my daughter, regularly body shaming her and continually preventing her from holding or being near her new baby sister. I felt completely helpless and trapped. I felt there was no way out.

It took more police involvement and me paying him a huge lump sum of money for Phil to finally leave. But the abuse continued. He used our child as a pawn against me. It was all too familiar: I had been through this with the father of my first two children. This time, it was worse. Phil was an insidious nightmare of a man who put me through more hell than I ever could have imagined. He insisted that we meet for his scheduled access visits with our child in a dark, deserted parking lot of a closed business. He would not hand over our infant daughter until he was finished talking to me. Talking was usually yelling and name calling while he held our vulnerable baby in his arms.

He insisted on a schedule of four to eight pm on Tuesday and Thursday one week and Monday and Wednesday the following, plus every other weekend. As our child got older, Phil refused to adapt to the schedule to allow me to enroll her in the sports and activities our child loved. I finally convinced him to allow me to register our child in summer swimming lessons but then he called the police to report that I breached the court order and prevented him from having scheduled court-ordered access—despite our written arrangement. He did this three times and the police decided to charge me with breach of a court order.

I had never been charged with anything in my life and being arrested may have been the most terrifying thing I have ever gone through. I had never been more scared in my life and was so worried about the consequences of having a criminal record. Having to go into the OPP basement where I was fingerprinted and had mug shots taken. I had to attend criminal court. All because I had taken my child to a mutually agreed upon swimming lesson, for which he'd given written consent.

By this point, I was receiving counseling. My counselor referred me to a social worker at the YWCA shelter. The social worker attended the first court date with me and set me up with a lawyer. During my first meeting with the lawyer, he contacted the crown attorney and had the charge against me dropped. Both he and the crown were shocked that the police placed a criminal charge against me for an apparent breach of a family court order. I filed a complaint against the police officer that charged me. An investigation took place, and they shredded my fingerprints in front of me to dramatically show they had dropped the charges. Although that was what I wanted, it didn't come close to making up all I had gone through. And there were no consequences for the police officer or for Phil.

I am sharing my story with you because I want you to notice that I kept making the same choice in men. My path and choice of partners did not change until I got help. Lots of help. Through the help I sought out and received, I learned that because of my shitty childhood, I was drawn to men like my abusive stepfather. I was conditioned to choose "that" type of man as a partner. Before I received counseling, every single man I was with was abusive in some way. I needed to work on myself to realize my part in enabling their behavior and for choosing that type of man in the first place.

Through counseling, I learned about protecting myself by establishing boundaries, and became aware of how shockingly few I had. I had in some ways trained my exes to treat me badly. I used to just pick up their plates, pick up after them, and when you set a precedent of behavior, it's hard to change them afterwards. For example, my first husband, Robert, would come back from work and just look at me. I knew what the look meant. I would stop whatever I was doing and get his dinner on the table.

Once I was outside of these relationships, I was led by my fear of being alone and was never single for longer than a couple of weeks. I thrived on co-dependent relationships without boundaries. The healing for me started with individual counseling and then group therapy. I also read lots of books about relationships and mental illnesses.

Group therapy was really hard, but I think it was the most important part of my recovery. I benefited from being with other women who had similar or even worse experiences than my own as I could relate to their stories. I learned about all of the unhealthy relationship patterns that we can fall into through the examples of other women and together we learned about how to create healthy, loving relationships. I graduated from the group and moved on to become one of the group facilitators. I loved that I could give back and help women who were where I once was.

When I think back to how lost I was and how close I was to being in a woman's shelter myself, I feel *so* lucky and grateful that I made it past those dark days. I spent almost three years on my own, working on myself before I dared to even *consider* dating. After this, when

I was ready, I met Tom, my current husband who is a good man and a supportive husband. He is nothing like any man that I have previously been with. I see him as an enhancement of my life rather than a necessity.

Now we have been together for over twelve wonderful years and our relationship gets better with each passing year. Tom is kind; he is a great father, and we are now grandparents. Plus, he gave me a bonus stepdaughter whom I have had the pleasure of raising since she was three. He often says that he wishes we had met when we were younger and although I may wish I had been with him all along, it is horrible to acknowledge this, but I know that I would not have chosen him back then. And I was a different person—and truthfully, he may not have wanted that version of me either. Before I could create the loving relationship we have, I needed to do the work on myself. I had to make changes in order to achieve the healthy relationship that I am blessed to have today.

As I reflect on my history of violent and abusive partners and compare that life to the calm and peace that is my life now, it is hard to acknowledge, but it is so true that I was a large contributor to my own unhappiness. Back then, I felt my problems were Doug then Robert then Joseph, then Phil. I felt blameless. They were clearly the bad guys. But it was me who allowed them into my heart and my home. I forgive myself for that. As Maya Angelou famously said, "Do the best you can until you know better. Then when you know better, do better."

When you can accept responsibility for your bad choices, you can learn to set up and enforce boundaries so that making good choices is easier. This was the biggest step in my recovery. I hope women reading this will be inspired to reflect on their choices and to truly embody their ability to create the lives they deserve for themselves and for their children.

Help Her
RECOVER

The present moment is the only moment available to us, and it is the door to all moments.

~ *Thich Nhat Hanh*

Help Her RECOVER

By Amanda Willett

PRESENCE Principle 5: "I WORK TOWARD PRESENCE IN MY BODY" emphasizes the importance of reconnecting with one's body as a crucial aspect of healing from gender-based violence. Survivors often endure physical and emotional trauma that can lead to disconnection from their own bodies. This principle encourages survivors to engage in practices like yoga, meditation, or therapy that foster a deeper connection to their physical selves. By acknowledging and addressing the physical and emotional scars left by their experiences, survivors can gradually regain a sense of control, self-compassion, and a feeling of safety within their bodies. It highlights the idea that healing involves not just the mind but also the body, allowing survivors to reclaim their physical presence, strength, and resilience as they continue their path to recovery.

Angela Baltkois journey is a powerful testament to the importance of being present in one's body, understanding the impact of past trauma, and learning to set healthy boundaries. From a young age, Angela faced abuse, abandonment, and toxic relationships. She struggled with abusive boyfriends and partners who controlled her life.

The theme of "presence in her body" is illustrated in Angela's journey towards self-awareness and healing. She initially found herself in a cycle of abusive relationships, which she attributes to her challenging childhood and low self-esteem. However, as she sought help through individual and group therapy, Angela began to recognize her own role in these patterns. She discovered that she needed to work on herself and set boundaries to break free from these toxic relationships.

Angela's story serves as an inspiring example of personal growth and healing. She learned to take responsibility for her choices and worked on building her self-worth. Ultimately, she found a loving and supportive partner in Tom, which marked a significant transformation in her life.

Her narrative highlights her journey towards "presence in one's body" through self-reflection, healing, and the establishment of healthy boundaries. Her story is a testament to the resilience of survivors of gender-based violence and their ity for growth and change.

PRESENCE

Principle 5:
I WORK TOWARD PRESENCE IN MY BODY

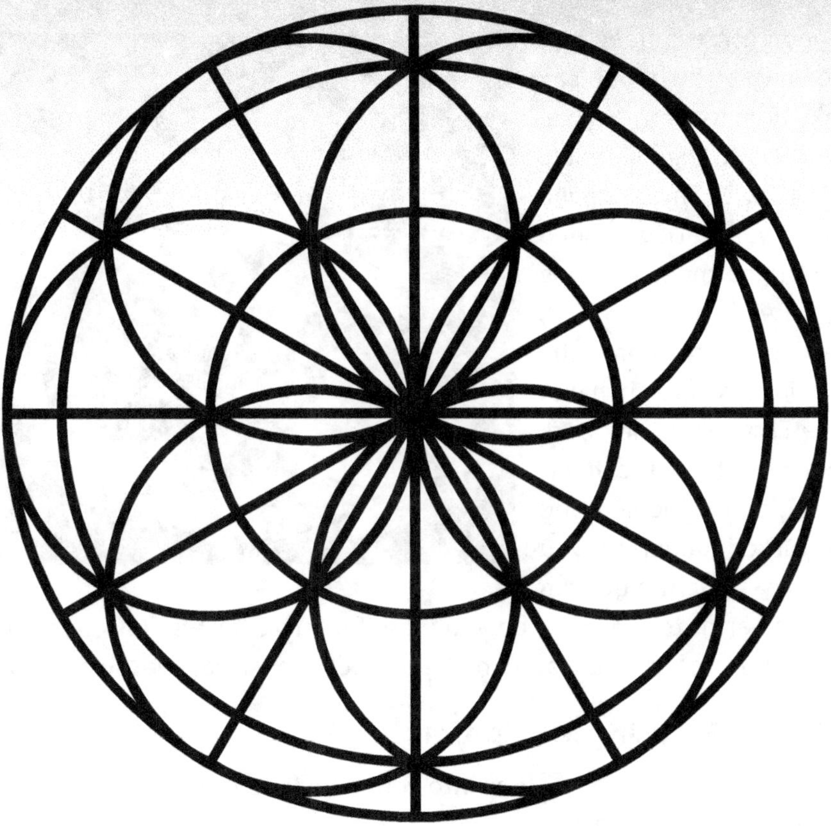

Explore the concept of "body wisdom."
What insights or guidance has your body provided to you in the past, and how can you learn to trust and listen to it more deeply?

Affirmation:

My body is a vessel of wisdom, and I listen to its signals with love and care.

Pigeon Pose kapotasana

Pigeon offers a deep hip-opening stretch but can take time to learn to love. To get into Pigeon, you'll start in Three-Legged Downward Dog. Bend your right knee and bring it forward to the floor, resting it behind or at the outside of your right hand. Stretch your left leg back and rest it on the floor, toes pointed behind you or tucked under as you remain upright you can lift your arms to the sky or do a forward fold. You can also lower down to your forearms or forehead to make this pose more passive. Switch sides.

Mindful Focusing Meditation:

This practice will help you tune into your body's sensations and messages with compassion and attentiveness:

Find a Quiet Space: Begin by finding a quiet and comfortable place to sit or lie down. Ensure you won't be disturbed during your meditation.

RITUALS FOR Recovery

Comfortable Posture: Sit or lie in a relaxed and comfortable position. Close your eyes if you're comfortable doing so or keep them gently focused on a spot in front of you.

Begin with Deep Breaths: Start with a few deep breaths to relax. Inhale deeply through your nose, allowing your lungs to fill completely, and exhale slowly through your mouth, releasing any tension with each breath.

Body Scan: Bring your attention to different parts of your body, starting from your toes and moving gradually upward. As you focus on each part, take a moment to notice any sensations, tension, or discomfort.

Listen to Your Body: As you scan your body, practice listening to it attentively. When you encounter areas of tension or discomfort, breathe into those areas with gentleness. Imagine your breath soothing and releasing any tension.

Mindful Breathing: Shift your focus to your breath. Feel the rhythm of your breath as it flows in and out of your body. Imagine your breath carrying love and care to every cell of your body.

Body's Wisdom: Reflect on the idea that your body is a vessel of wisdom. It carries the knowledge of your experiences and emotions. Visualize this wisdom as a warm, radiant light within you.

Non-Judgmental Awareness: As you continue to breathe mindfully, be aware of any thoughts or judgments that arise about your body. Instead of judging, offer yourself love and acceptance. Remind yourself that your body has always done its best to support you.

Gratitude: Take a moment to express gratitude for your body and the wisdom it holds. Think about all the things your body allows you to do and experience in life. Cultivate a sense of appreciation for your body's resilience.

Affirmations: Repeat the following affirmations to yourself with Sincerity: "My body is a vessel of wisdom.""I listen to my body's signals with love and care.""I am grateful for the wisdom my body provides."

Silence and Stillness: Spend a few moments in silence, simply observing your breath and the sensations in your body. Allow yourself to be fully present in this moment, appreciating the wisdom your body offers.

Closing: When you're ready to conclude the meditation, take a few deep breaths. Gently move your fingers and toes. Open your eyes if they were closed. Carry this sense of love, care, and attentiveness to your body into your daily life.

This mindful meditation practice encourages you to honor your body as a vessel of wisdom and cultivate a loving and caring relationship with it. Regularly listening to your body's signals with compassion can lead to greater self-awareness and well-being.

SPEAK OUT

ERIN HELLIER

Erin experienced emotional, psychological, mental, financial, sexual, and physical abuse in her marriage. She left with nothing; not even her son. Years later a wonderful yoga teacher introduced her to Rituals for Recovery, and this is where my healing journey began. Erin learned about narcissistic abuse and its long-lasting effects. She started therapy and learned about CPTSD, which can be caused by years of experiencing narcissistic abuse. After learning about trauma-responsive mind-body healing and somatics Erin is now on her way to becoming a Trauma Responsive Mind Body Wellness And SEL Somatic Teacher to help others to begin to heal.

Erin resides in Peterborough Ontario and is a dental receptionist and a full-time single mom.

SURVIVING AN OLYMPIC-LEVEL NARCISSIST

By
Erin Hellier

You may not control all the events that happen to you, but you can decide not to be reduced by them.

—Maya Angelou

I still remember the first time I knew my husband was lying to me. I was five or six months pregnant with our son. As I watched him flailing about in the lake water in front of our beautiful cottage, I wondered where this man's swimming skills had gone. After all, he told me he had almost made the British Olympic diving team. I even questioned him on it. He looked at me as if baffled, claiming he had never said any such thing to me. "Why would I say that?" he asked me. "It isn't even true!"

Was I remembering what he'd told me incorrectly or making things up again? This time I was sure I was not, so I took it further. I checked in with my parents; I knew they had been there when he made this claim. They remembered, too. This confirmed it: he was lying. But for the life of me, I couldn't figure out why. I brushed this incident off and turned a blind eye, much like I had with his other silly lies, so far.

This wasn't the first time he had called me crazy and asked what was wrong with my brain. By this point, it was a regular occurrence for me. It was an extremely stressful number of years as we had purchased a pharmacy; we were struggling to make the business work. I was up all hours of the day and night, working seven days a week. I was sleep deprived and completely stressed out. I brushed off my memory lapses as being due to anxiety and stress. However, this was the first time I could prove to myself that I'd been lied to; I had reliable witnesses that corroborated it.

Things were not always this way in our marriage. When I first met my husband, I was a tender twenty-four-year-old young woman. He was thirty-nine, almost forty and married with two children. His marriage, he told me, was at the end and had been for a long time. His wife was aware of this, he said. He told me he was staying in the relationship for his children and because his wife was sick with a tumor in her pituitary gland. I am not sure why, but he boasted he had cheated on her numerous times because they were not intimate anymore. "She's crazy," he said many times.

I, of course, found out later this was not the case whatsoever. Family and friends were shocked when he left his wife, as was she. I was so young and naïve back then. I never questioned his version of his marriage or doubted the integrity of his intentions with me.

We had a whirlwind, heavy romance. On our first weekend trip away, he bought me an expensive watch and claimed he had never felt this way about anybody. He said he was overwhelmed by his feelings for me. He couldn't wait for us to move in together and start a brand-new life. I thought I was the luckiest girl alive. This older, attractive, affluent man with a gorgeous British accent liked me! Never mind that he was my very senior boss in the busy pharmacy chain where we both worked. Because of the work situation, this relationship meant he was putting his job on the line for me: how romantic! And when it was discovered that a married executive manager was having an affair with an entry-level employee, things got very strained at work. At the time, I believed he risked everything and quit that job out of love for me.

Things progressed very quickly. In a matter of months, he moved into my one-bedroom, basement apartment. By this point, he had franchised a busy pharmacy and hired me to work there. And then, less than a year into our relationship, he asked me to marry him.

I was twenty-five years old. I knew the engagement was coming because he had made a big production about taking me ring shopping and getting a custom-made ring. He proposed to me in the middle of the pharmacy one night and of course I said yes. He took the ring back after that, however, so he could stage a "proper" proposal at a restaurant in front of all the patrons. Red flags were already apparent by this time; however, I was too blind to see them as such. Perhaps I just did not want to acknowledge them.

We had a fairy tale wedding. It was the most stressful time of my life. I was planning a wedding completely on my own whilst working sixty to seventy hours per week in our new pharmacy. All our friends and family came; it was an amazing day. There is one incident, however, that stands out. Just before my parents walked me down the aisle, my mother turned to me and told me that I didn't have to do this. I will admit, I was a bit confused. Sure, I had seen Paul's temper and the cycle of abuse had already started; I just wasn't aware of it as a "cycle." I thought the behavior he was exhibiting was normal; after all, he was even more stressed than I was with the business. But this moment shows my mother saw the man he was. This was her way of gently trying to warn me. I should have heeded her warning.

*   *   *

We became the sole owners of our pharmacy after our business partner passed away very tragically. I was alarmed when he took the business right out from under our partner's widow, in her most vulnerable moments. He justified his actions, telling me that she would have used this opportunity to take the business away from us if he hadn't acted first. It was only business, he said. By this point, my husband was using drugs frequently: both stealing them from the pharmacy and buying them from our methadone customers. He was always angry and disgusted with me because I didn't agree with his treatment of our business partner's widow and because of the obvious signs of my difficulty dealing with the challenges of our business.

The College of Pharmacists launched an investigation into the business, and my husband believed the best way to thwart this investigation was to sell it. He was right; with the sale, the investigation stopped. We made a lot of money and used it to buy a beautiful home on a lake in Eastern Ontario. It should have been a dream. I got pregnant around this time and thought our life would be changing as the stress of managing the pharmacy was gone. We could live a simple life. My parents moved in with us, staying in the in-law suite attached to our house. Little did I know the worst years of my life were ahead of me.

As my husband had over-extended our finances; we couldn't live the retired life he had promised. Instead, he went searching for a new pharmacy to purchase. He found one less than an hour away from us. The woman who previously owned it was dying and needed to sell. My husband made himself look like a nice and sympathetic man who would surely look after her employees.

With the sale completed, it was again full throttle with a new business. I was not having an easy pregnancy; I was often nauseous and physically sick. That did not matter to my husband. I had to go in to work every single day, carrying around a garbage can as I frequently needed to throw. I was completely miserable. How, our staff would ask, did I put up with him? Like my mother, they could clearly see him for what he was. I, however, was still blind. It's just business, I would say, parroting what he would tell me.

I had an emergency Caesarean section and was in the hospital for eight days due to complications. It was a very scary time. The day after

I came home, my husband forced me back to work. I couldn't take the time off, he said; the business was falling apart without me there. I went back, stitches and all, while he sat at home in bed because he was simply too exhausted from working while I had been "laying around" in the hospital. Unsurprisingly, I developed depression. I had a hard time pulling myself out of bed and taking care of our son. Thankfully my parents were there and able to step in and help.

My husband had been getting more and more nasty during this time, calling me fat, lazy, stupid, and claiming nobody else would ever want me. This was interspersed with periods of him being so apologetic, buying flower and gifts to apologize, telling me he loved me so much. At these times he would say, "I just have a hard time controlling my temper and emotions, but I love you so much." I forgave him time and time again.

I started developing symptoms of a severe mental health condition. I know now it is CPTSD—Complex Post Traumatic Stress Disorder. At the time, however, I had no idea what was wrong with me. My husband at first claimed that I must have post-partum depression, then he decided I was bipolar. He pointed out I had periods where I couldn't sleep, I was constantly on edge, I had started to lose my grip on what was real and what was not. He toyed with the idea that maybe I had early onset Alzheimer's. I knew something was wrong with me, I just didn't know what, so I accepted his views on this.

I also didn't know what a narcissist or narcissistic abuse was. I didn't know many other psychiatric and psychology terms I would soon become familiar with including love bombing, gas lighting, and breadcrumbing. I didn't know that it was going to get worse before it got better. I just knew that the man I loved, and who I thought loved me, was telling me I was losing my mind. I believed him because the alternative of him being abusive was too much for me to comprehend at that point.

My doctors put me on some pretty heavy hitting medications: Cipralex, lorazepam, quetiapine, lithium. You name it, I was on it.

I was also on pain medications due to a badly herniated disc in my back, which I ended up "needing" surgery for. My husband could not wait for physio to work as he decided that treatment was taking me away from work for too long. I was walking with a cane and in a lot of pain. My husband pushed me to tell the doctor that I was becoming incontinent due to my injury so they would do the surgery. This was untrue; however, the alternative of having my husband scream and yell at me for not going to work was unbearable. Surgery seemed like the kinder alternative for me. I was walking around in a fog. I was heavily medicated and very confused.

My husband used my confusion as an excuse to attend doctor appointments with me. He would explain "what was really happening" and the doctors accepted his version of me. As a medical professional himself, every doctor he spoke with believed his explanation of everything. I was no help to myself as I didn't know what was going on by this point. Why couldn't I remember things he said he told me? Why was I confused and constantly getting things I could remember mixed up? Nothing was making any sense. The doctors increased my medications to near maximum doses because they were not working for me.

Things began to become more than the emotional and mental abuse I had been experiencing. This is when I knew for certain that I was being abused. He threw a cell phone at my head, pinned me down, and took my bank cards from me. He pushed me down the stairs, chased me around with a two by four when I tried to leave, and various other violent situations that arose left no doubt in my mind that he was the root of my difficulties, not some organic mental illness. I was afraid and called the police several times. The first time was when he choked my father for standing up for me. He did this in front of our son. I had to jump on his back and fight him off. I will never forget the look in his eyes: it was pure madness, yet I could not disentangle myself from the situation.

Eventually, we had to sell our second pharmacy as well. My husband stole hundreds of narcotics from the pharmacy and the college was closing in. Again, he sold to avoid the investigation. He lied repeatedly and had me lying on his behalf as well. Don't tell the truth, he told me. Did I want to lose everything we had worked for? Did I want him to end up in jail? Did I want my son to grow up without a father or any means of support? I had no real education and no job experience other than pharmacy, he reminded me. I would ruin everything if I spoke the truth. I kept quiet and lied for him and even took the blame when he finally got caught in his schemes. I thought that was loyalty.

Things progressed at home to the point where he was regularly telling me I should kill myself because I was so useless. He even went so far to hand me a straight razor and tell me to slit my wrists. His verbal abuse was nearly constant by this point. I had zero sexual attraction to him anymore, but he would sit beside me in bed and berate me, telling me it was my duty to have sex with him. It didn't matter if I liked it, I just had to lay there and take it. If I refused, he would masturbate furiously next to me. I would eventually give in, just so he would stop. On occasion, he would just force me to have sex with him against my will. I still have a hard time acknowledging that was rape.

I checked myself in for a seventy-two-hour stay in the Brockville psychiatric unit as I was at my wits end and felt I was losing my mind. We discussed ECT for my depression. Luckily, my parents stepped in before we proceeded with this. I was ready to do anything by this point; I just wanted to stop feeling the way that I was feeling. It was explained to me that I was having an adverse effect to the quetiapine that I was taking; I still believe this was my brain's way of telling me that I did not need this medication. The quetiapine was stopped, and the lithium was increased. I was far from being better.

We ended up having to move. He had blown through all of our money with his expensive renovations of our cottage. We were broke; the only way out was to sell our home to pay off our debts. I was heartbroken. The life I had been promised was gone. It had been gone for years but somehow having to sell our home solidified it for me. I was under no illusions anymore; I knew with certainty that I was being abused. I still didn't, however, understand the scope of it.

After we moved, things somehow got even worse. I felt trapped in my marriage because, even if I could figure out a plan to leave, my husband would not let me take our son with me. I was severely mentally ill, he told me, and couldn't be trusted with our child. Children's Aid Society (CAS) was involved at this point, due to a neighbor calling to report us because of our loud and constant fighting. The CAS social workers also believed my husband when he told them I was severely bipolar.

I left in the end because I was afraid for my life; leaving without my son was the hardest thing I have ever done. My husband was becoming more and more unhinged and unpredictable in his fits of rage. I was certain I was going to end up dead, or severely injured. I left although I knew my husband was continuing the cycle of abuse with our child, constantly commenting on his weight, yet he was just five years old. He yelled at him all the time, saying he was "misbehaving." After I left, my husband fed our child lies, telling him I left for no reason except to break the family apart; I was selfish and didn't care about them.

I had to tread very carefully around my husband to ensure he would allow me access to our son. Any act of defiance that suggested to him I did not accept his version of the situation resulted in him withholding our son from me. The abuse was far from over even though I had left. Now he had the perfect weapon, the thing I loved most in the world, and he held it over me every chance he got. Eventually, though, he got tired of having our son most of the time. It was too much work for him. He eventually agreed to shared custody. I was thrilled. This, however, brought a whole new set of challenges.

I got numerous calls from the school that nobody had picked up our son when school was finished. My husband would call me saying he was just too busy to pick him up, and could I do it? Our son would come to my house with rotten lunches and looking exhausted. I didn't know what to do or who to turn to. It was written in our contract with CAS that I was mentally ill. My now estranged husband still had full access to my medical doctors to discuss my treatment because he had them convinced I could not be trusted to be honest with them about my mental state. No doctor believed me; my husband had made sure of this.

The pandemic then hit. I know this was a horrible time in many people's lives, but it turned out to be the biggest blessing for my son and I. I was laid off from my job working nights at the casino, however, my husband and his new fiancée both worked in healthcare. As "essential service providers" they continued to work. When my husband decided I should be the primary caregiver for our son, I was ecstatic even though he would dictate when and where he would see our son. Most of the time, he wouldn't show up, would show up late, or would drop our son off to me early. My "off" time was not my own as it was constantly invaded by his ever-changing mind, but at least I had my son.

I attended a virtual conference through the charity Rituals for Recovery, the publisher of this book, about a year into the pandemic. One of the speakers spoke about narcissistic abuse. A lightbulb went off in my brain: she could have been telling my story. I was overwhelmed when I realized the scope of what I had experienced.

It was no wonder that I was not healing from my marriage. Not only was the abuse still ongoing, but I was still on medications for a condition that I now knew I did not have. I was not bipolar, I had CPTSD. I didn't need lithium, I needed therapy. Still, it took me a while longer to truly accept all of this. At first I thought that since I now knew what was wrong with me, I could just deal with it on my own. I was very wrong.

My Rituals for Recovery

I had been living in my fight of flight response for so many years, I didn't know how to function any other way. I was constantly triggered and very, very angry. There was no rest and relaxation in my life. There was fear, anger, sadness, and denial. It was very hard for me to accept that the man I loved had systematically abused me since day one. The man I loved had never loved me and didn't know how to love. I needed professional help in many ways. I needed a lawyer, a therapist, and I was sure there were other types of help I needed that I was unaware of. I didn't know where to start.

Someone at Rituals for Recovery suggested I check out the free legal support available through the government's Legal Aid programs for survivors of abuse. I started gathering pamphlets and scouring all their online materials. The second resource they suggested was the Barbra Schlifer Commemorative Clinic in my nearest big city, Toronto. They are a great resource for women who have left abusive relationships and don't know where to start looking for help. I'm sure they have similar agencies in other big cities.

Locally I contacted my YWCA, who suggested places that I could go to start therapy. I was not, however, ready for therapy. The thought of rehashing what had happened to me was too much for me to deal with. They did, however, connect me with a lawyer with who agreed to take on my case.

At the time of writing, I am still in the court process, which is still slowed down due to the backlog of cases after the pandemic. It hasn't helped that my estranged husband hasn't filed his taxes in a number of years and has been unable to provide financial information to the courts. However, the feeling of empowerment that I felt filing court documents stating the instances of abuse I suffered at his hands is almost indescribable. Telling the horrors of my marriage made the shame I had go away. Telling my story to others and seeing the reactions from them has been validating. I am not crazy. I was never crazy. I was abused in ways that nobody should ever have to experience. I was not weak, in fact, quite the opposite. I had strength beyond what even I could comprehend.

Eventually I connected with a therapist through Rituals for Recovery. Therapy has been beyond a lifesaver for me. Therapy is not easy. It is a lot of going back in time and reliving the trauma that has been experienced. It was sleepless nights and crying; guilt and shame coming back up; blaming myself for staying so long. It was not knowing where to begin in my story and wondering how I was ever going to heal from my trauma. I truly thought I was beyond help. I felt what I had experienced was too much for any one person to deal with. My therapist is amazing. She helped me to unpack my past and process my grief.

I needed to grieve my relationship. This process was extremely helpful to me. It helped to let go of my past and let go of what I thought my life was supposed to look like. I began to accept what had happened to me. I stopped looking at it as something I had caused. My feelings of guilt and anger slowly began to fade away. I became kinder to current self, but also to my past self. I did what I thought was best at the time in the circumstances I had been handed. I learned techniques such as the 5, 4, 3, 2, 1 method, meditating, ice baths, journaling—all tools to help me cope with my trauma. I learned how to manage triggers and to take time to process my emotions. Prior to this, many of my emotions came out as anger. Through therapy I discovered that I was rarely actually angry. I was sad, frustrated, and overwhelmed, but not angry. Taking the time to process what I was actually feeling before reacting has made me a better mother, and a better person.

Yoga also played a huge role in my healing. I had been practicing yoga for a number of years but became more serious in my practice during the pandemic. I began to let the healing effects of yoga take over, rather than just practicing it for the physical aspects. I let my mind and body become free rather than focusing on whether I was doing the poses correctly. The healing aspects of collective breathing and the mind/body connection were very powerful for me. Yoga was one of the first activities that truly brought me solace and peace of mind. As I became more accepting of my emotions, I realized I was beginning to attract like-minded individuals into my life. As an empath, I have always attracted people into my life in some form. People always love to tell me their problems and life stories. I decided it was time to tap into this aspect of my personality.

Rituals for Recovery offered a trauma informed yoga teacher certification and I decided to do it to expand my own knowledge for my own well-being. I wasn't sure how I would cope with it. I had my son full time and I worked full time. I try to work out five days a week, plus meditate, and meal plan. The yoga program seemed like a lot to take on but Amanda, our inspirational leader at Rituals for Recovery, has made this process so accommodating for all. There is no pressure for timelines, recordings are available of all the teachings, and there is no pressure to be perfect. What I found was a community of like-minded individuals, most if not all had experienced some trauma, and we are all trying to use our individual experiences to make change in a world filled with survivors of trauma.

I now plan to teach yoga, to offer smaller group classes and really focus on the healing that yoga can offer. I want to show people that healing is possible for everybody. It is not an easy road, and it is not a linear path, but it is possible. I want to volunteer my time with the vulnerable homeless population in my city and try to make any sort of difference that I can. I truly believe we are all capable of healing from our past traumas—we just need the proper supports to be able to do so. Building community and connecting with individuals who understand how to deal with trauma is essential to healing. Something I have learned is that we are not our trauma. We do not have to let it negatively affect the rest of our lives. Trauma can be used for good once you have taken the steps to heal.

My story could have had a much different ending. There were times and I was ready to give up. It certainly would have been much easier to never deal with what had happened to me and continue to live in anger and anxiety. In my own way, in the years after leaving my husband, I was a toxic person. It took a lot for me to accept this.

I was barely getting through life. I had no intimate connections with anybody. I could not trust anybody. I still struggle to trust. I have one thing now, however, that I didn't have before: hope. I see the light at the end of the tunnel. I am finally happy with my life and what it became. I am grateful that I had the constant support of my friends and family, even when I was difficult to deal with. Having a support system is paramount to healing. I hope to be part of others' support systems.

My healing continues and will continue for the rest of my life. I have many tools at my disposal to deal with the not-so-good days. I don't let them overtake me and rule my life. I still have triggers, nightmares, doubts, and fears. I do not believe they will ever go away; however, now they are manageable. Journaling in the morning after a night of bad dreams helps me to let go of the negative emotions I experience and move on to have a productive day. Sitting and meditating when I'm overwhelmed allows me to re-center and re-ground my thoughts and feelings. I have learned EFT tapping techniques, the benefits and dance and art therapy, the healing aspects of drumming circles, and using *pranayama* (breathing exercises) to ground my thoughts and emotions.

I have accepted that I will never become the girl I was before the abuse. I used to believe the goal of healing was to get back to my former self. I realize now that she is gone, but what I can become now is so much more. None of this would have been possible without experiencing the trauma in my life. I sometimes miss her and the carefree way she lived her life. She was so trusting and naïve. She also carried me through the trauma in my life in ways that I could never imagine. She became strong and helped me to turn into the woman I am today. I am a strong, independent, self-sufficient woman. I know I can get through anything now because I survived the worst thing that could have happened to me.

There is hope for everybody. People do truly want to help you to recover. I want to use my voice to bring awareness to narcissistic abuse and its devastating effects on those who experience it.

Help Her RECOVER

In recovery, I've learned that acknowledging and processing my emotions is the true path to healing.

~ *Demi Lovato*

Help Her RECOVER

By Amanda Willett

FEELING Principle 6: "I FEEL SO THAT I CAN HEAL" recognizes the significance of acknowledging and processing one's emotions as an essential step in recovering from gender-based violence. Survivors often grapple with a complex array of emotions, including fear, anger, shame, and grief, stemming from their traumatic experiences. This principle encourages survivors to confront these emotions, whether through therapy, support groups, or self-reflection, to gradually heal. By allowing themselves to feel and express these emotions, survivors can gradually release the emotional burdens they carry and work towards a healthier mental and emotional state. It underscores the idea that healing involves confronting and embracing one's emotions rather than suppressing them, paving the way for personal growth, resilience, and the restoration of emotional well-being.

Erin Hellier's story begins with her relationship with a much older, married man who initially swept her off her feet. Over time, she realized that her husband was a narcissist who manipulated and abused her both mentally and physically. As she navigated through the challenges of a troubled marriage, her mental and emotional health deteriorated. She experienced memory lapses, confusion, and was diagnosed with various mental health conditions, all of which were misrepresented by her husband.

The story illustrates the devastating impact of narcissistic abuse on one's mental health, self-esteem, and overall well-being. Erin's journey towards healing involves several important elements, including:

Awareness: Erin eventually recognized that she was in an abusive relationship, a crucial first step in her healing process.

Seeking Professional Help: She connected with therapists and support organizations, acknowledging that she needed profes- sional assistance to address her trauma and mental health challenges.

Community Support: Erin found support from organizations like Rituals for Recovery and the Barbra Schlifer Commemorative Clinic, as well as through legal aid programs. These resources helped her navigate the legal system and access therapeutic support.

Therapy and Self-Reflection: Through therapy, Erin learned to process her trauma, manage her emotions, and reframe her understanding of herself. She discovered tools like yoga, meditation, and journaling to cope with her emotions.

Empowerment: Erin found strength in sharing her story and seeking justice through the legal system. Speaking out about her experiences allowed her to shed the shame and guilt that had plagued her for so long.

Advocacy: She aspires to become a trauma-informed yoga teacher and help others heal from their traumas. Erin emphasizes the importance of building a supportive community of survivors and advocates to facilitate healing.

Erin's story ultimately conveys a message of hope and resilience. Despite enduring years of abuse, she has found a path to healing and aims to use her voice to raise awareness about narcissistic abuse and its effects. Erin exemplifies the theme of Principle 6, "I FEEL SO THAT I CAN HEAL," by highlighting the importance of acknowledging one's feelings, seeking help, and actively participating in the journey toward recovery.

FEELING

Principle 6:
I FEEL SO THAT I CAN HEAL

Describe a recent moment of emotional insight or clarity. What did you learn about yourself through this experience?

Are there any past emotional wounds or traumas that you've been avoiding or suppressing?

Affirmation:

Feeling is my superpower, helping me to heal and thrive in every aspect of my life.

Bridge Pose

Bridge Pose is great for stretching out areas of your body you don't often think of stretching, like the abdomen and chest, as well as building strength in your legs, glutes, and back. To get into Bridge, lie down on your back and place your feet flat on the floor at a comfortable distance from your hips. Place your arms flat at your sides, pressing your shoulders and back into your mat as you lift your hips up. Engage your inner thighs and root down through the soles of your feet.

Mindful Focusing Meditation:

This practice will help you embrace and harness the power of your emotions for healing and personal growth:

Find a Quiet Space:

Begin by finding a quiet and comfortable place to sit or lie down. Ensure you won't be disturbed during your meditation.

Comfortable Posture: Sit or lie in a relaxed and comfortable position. Close your eyes if you're comfortable doing so or keep them gently focused on a spot in front of you.

Deep Breaths: Start with a few deep breaths to relax. Inhale deeply through your nose, allowing your lungs to fill completely, and exhale slowly through your mouth, releasing any tension with each breath.

Awareness of Emotions: Bring your attention to your emotions. Notice how you're feeling in this moment without judgment. Are there any emotions present? Are they subtle or strong? Acknowledge whatever you're feeling.

Breathe into Emotions: As you breathe, imagine that you're breathing into the core of your emotions. Picture your breath as a warm, healing light that surrounds and soothes your feelings. Let your breath embrace your emotions with gentleness.

Superpower Visualization: Visualize your emotions as vibrant, colorful energy within you. See them as your superpower, a force that can guide you, heal you, and help you thrive. Each emotion has a unique color and quality.

Connect with Emotions: Take a moment to connect with each emotion you're experiencing. Name them silently or out loud. For example, "I feel happiness, I feel sadness, I feel gratitude." Acknowledge and honor each emotion.

Healing Breath: With each breath, imagine your emotions becoming more balanced and harmonious. See any negative emotions gradually transforming into positive, empowering ones. Visualize this transformation with clarity.

Affirmations: Repeat the following affirmations to yourself with sincerity:

"Feeling is my superpower." "My emotions guide me towards healing and growth." "I embrace and honor my feelings in every aspect of my life."

Embrace Sensations: Shift your focus to the physical sensations associated with your emotions. Notice if there's tension, warmth, or any other sensation in your body. Allow these sensations to be present without resistance.

Healing Light: Imagine a radiant light glowing within you, representing the healing power of your emotions. See this light spreading throughout your body, revitalizing and strengthening you.

Silence and Stillness: Spend a few moments in silence, observing your emotions, sensations, and the rhythm of your breath. Be fully present in this moment, appreciating the superpower of your feelings.

Closing: When you're ready to conclude the meditation, take a few deep breaths. Gently move your fingers and toes. Open your eyes if they were closed. Carry this sense of emotional empowerment and healing into your daily life.

This mindful meditation practice encourages you to embrace your emotions as a superpower that can guide you toward healing and thriving. By acknowledging and working with your feelings, you can harness their energy for personal growth and well-being.

SPEAK OUT

TIWONGE GONDWE

Tiwonge was a subsistence farmer before she took up activism; she works to improve the lives of people living with HIV, the virus causing Aquired Immune Deficiency Syndrom (AIDS). She represents her home, Malawi, in regional and international conferences, without sacrificing her support for those with the virus at the community and national level.

Left to raise seven children in a society where ignorance and fear about HIV and AIDS were rising faster than infection rates, Tiwonge overcame the shame and poverty of being a young widow with HIV, eventually forming her own visionary team. Tiwonge and her organization have made great changes to culture and patriarchal practices in Malawi; her changes have influenced countries throughout Africa.

FROM SHAME AND POVERTY TO INTERNATIONAL RESPECT

By
Tiwonge Gondwe

You have to act as if it were possible to radically transform the world. And you have to do it all the time.

—Angela Davis

It was March 2000, and I was drowning in the misery of loss. I was standing in the sun but it was the judgement of my neighbours which burned hotter. My children and I stood with my husband's body as we were gathered to bury him. My mother had passed away only weeks earlier in February. I had to decide how I was going to survive and keep my own children and my mother's children together. I was thirty-four and now the caregiver of six children all under the age of eleven.

I did not know it then, but my neighbors were all convinced they knew that I was HIV positive. They did not attend the funeral and it was their obvious absences which burned me. Those who did come stood far away and I knew they had come more out of curiosity than concern. Plus in our patriarchal society as my mother had divorced and remarried again, the father of her youngest children was not the same as my own. Their father had abandoned them when he saw she was ill.

But I knew I could not keep them on my father's land. I had to find a different place for us all to live.

What would I do? Where would we end up?

Both my mother and my husband died due to HIV related diseases. I did not know at the time, but I was also HIV positive. I went to the hospital to get tested after the death of my husband and this was confirmed. Neighbours were already shunning me and gossiping. They were whispering that I was a whore and that I must have HIV. I was only barely able to feed myself and my own three children. Now I had six children and no other supports. The community was afraid of me as they believed they could catch death from me.

I had to find food for the children and save other food to sell to sustain the family. As people were gossiping and saying I was a bad woman, I decided to remarry in 2004. I thought it would bring security and make people think better of me, instead I put myself and my children in greater danger and instability.

It was an abusive marriage. I blamed myself for making this decision and putting my kids into more trauma. I was experiencing sexual violence, physical violence, and the man had extramarital affairs which emotionally abused me. He would take the products meant for sale to support the family and keep the money. There was economic abuse, and all of this was threatening the family and I was struggling to keep going. I was unable to make enough money for my family.

An NGO was looking for a local representative to educate people about HIV. They were looking for a leader who had HIV and was willing to talk about this. A gossiping neighbour went to and said, "she must be HIV positive because her husband had been sick and passed away." And I was also sick–I had shingles. Shingles makes you sick for a long time, and you develop sores so it is obvious to others. This is used against you, and I'd been in fear of how it would be used against me.

When offered the NGO position, I had no choice but to take it although I was so shamed by my marital situation and the gossip of my community. Before long, I realized just how important the work was. I was amazed at how good I was at it and I became a true activist. I received training in supporting women through the trauma of gender-based violence and learned how to protect them from acquiring HIV. If they had already acquired HIV, I taught them how to live safely and improve their health. I got people talking so that traditional practices which harmed women were criticized rather than accepted in order to protect women's health.

I thought: *As I'm an organizer, a head of this group of women, have been trained in GBV, and am a paralegal advisor, how can I stay in this abusive marriage?* I need to walk the walk as I was talking the talk and getting other women to stand up for themselves. I had to change the narrative for myself, my kids, and the community–to lead by example.

Working there emboldened me. That I could feed my children made me stronger and I saw that I had to stand up for my rights. I went to court and had them force my husband to leave the marital home. Then I divorced him.

I was leading many women and changing lives. Because of my direct work as well as the charity's, more women and men were coming out openly to start treatment for HIV using ARVs (anti-retroviral drugs). As we were mobilizing these women, we engaged our government so that they started providing free ARVs. Previously the drugs were available only privately and the government was saving them rather than distributing them.

My work led to changes in cultural practices which harmed women such as wife inheritance–if a husband died, the widow was forced to marry his brother or his relative. This was fuelling the increase in HIV and AIDs pandemic.

Discrimination in the community was also causing people to hide their status and thus infect others. Those with HIV were afraid to go to the doctor as they did not know they had a right to privacy; they were afraid to receive treatment as they worried even this could be discovered. They knew that, at that time, if people *even thought* you were HIV positive, you were stigmatized and not able to participate. You would be shunned, people would not associate with you, and you could lose your job.

Our work changed mindsets around HIV. We taught people you cannot stigmatize people by just by looking at them and deciding they are HIV positive. We taught people that no one has to disclosing their status. People began to understand that HIV could be treated and managed and that you could still have a good life. We taught people the many ways of preventing and spreading infections.

Learning and given an opportunity to lead changed my life. I received the treatment for HIV—the ARVs made me feel physically better because they reduce the amount of virus in your body until, for most people, it becomes so low you cannot transmit the virus to a sexual partner. It also stops HIV from attacking the cells in the body that fight off illness, thus you feel better. But there is no cure, so I knew, and I taught others, the importance of taking ARVs so they could have a long and healthy life.

However, dealing with shame is difficult. I worked with a type of therapy we call Positive Living Training. This helped me trust my strength and I could care for my children as I stopped thinking I was ill and dying. With ARVs I was not sick and with the training I started thinking differently. I could start planning and could do things without just being depressed.

Seeing how well it worked for me, I became excited about socializing others and creating groups. I created safe spaces where women who were HIV could meet, talk to each other, cook together, and sing. These things made me see there was life again and the bigger pleasure was doing this for others. Through our space, we also provided mediation and referral services for survivors of GBV, which is paramount to safety and improved health statuses.

Eventually I founded a women's forum called, Chikulamayembe. And I have represented my region and have been sent to represent my country at international conferences in various capacities. I am a leader who can strategize on subjects including HIV, the AIDs epidemic, GBV, and women's rights.

When my husband died and I was trying to feed six young children through subsistence farming, my main concern was what my neighbours would do when they discovered I was HIV positive. I was also sure, since I had HIV, that I would die any day leaving the children orphaned and abandoned. I am astounded at all I have achieved. I am a healthy leader who is globally respected for my work serving others. I have helped thousands upon thousands of women.

When I stood in the sun at my husband's funeral, I wondered what would become of me and all of my children. How would I house them and get them through school? Would I survive long enough to ensure they were safe? At that time, without a home, I could never imagine that one day I would build my own house—but I did!

And I am heartened to say I also managed to ensure all of my six children received a good education. They are now thriving adults and have given me many loving grandchildren. My heart is full.

Help Her RECOVER

Your life changes the moment you make a new, congruent, and committed decision.

~ *Tony Robbins*

Help Her RECOVER

By Amanda Willett

CHOICE Principle 7: "I CAN FIND CHOICE IN THE PRESENT MOMENT" is a guiding light for survivors of gender-based violence as they navigate their path to recovery. This principle empowers survivors to recognize that, even in the aftermath of trauma, they still possess the capacity to make choices in their lives. It encourages them to focus on the present moment, where they can exercise agency and make decisions that align with their healing journey. Whether it's seeking support, setting boundaries, or prioritizing self-care, survivors are reminded that they have the power to shape their own narrative and regain control over their lives. This principle promotes mindfulness and self-compassion, allowing survivors to gradually reclaim their sense of autonomy and build a future that is more aligned with their desires and values.

Tiwonge Gondwe's story begins with her facing immense challenges, having lost her husband and mother to HIV-related illnesses, leaving her as the caregiver for six children, including her own and her mother's. Despite the judgment and stigma from her neighbors who believed she was HIV positive, Tiwonge had to make choices to ensure the survival and well-being of her family.

She faced the harsh realities of social ostracism due to her HIV status, but she made the courageous choice to remarry in 2004, hoping to provide security for her family and change the community's perception of her. Unfortunately, this decision led to an abusive marriage, where she experienced various forms of violence and economic exploitation.

Tiwonge's life took a turning point when she was offered a position as a local representative for an NGO, advocating for HIV education and support. Despite the shame and gossip surrounding her, she accepted the role. Through this work, she discovered her talent for activism, especially in empowering women affected by gender-based violence (GBV) and HIV. She became an advocate for women's rights and worked to change cultural practices and stigma related to HIV.

This journey empowered Tiwonge, making her realize that she could not remain in an abusive marriage while advocating for the rights and well-being of others. She took legal action to have her husband leave.

Tiwonge's story demonstrates how, in the face of adversity and limited choices, she found opportunities to make positive choices in the present moment. Her work as an activist not only transformed her life but also the lives of many other women. She successfully challengedcultural norms, advocated for HIV treatment, and created safe spaces for survivors of GBV. Tiwonge's resilience and determination highlight the theme of finding choices and empowerment in the face of adversity.

CHOICE

Principle 7:
I CAN FIND CHOICE IN THE PRESENT MOMENT

Consider the relationship between past conditioning and present choices. Are there patterns from your past that influence your choices in the present?

How can you become more aware of these patterns?

Affirmation:

I am not limited by circumstances; I am empowered by the choices I make.

Downward Dog

You can do this pose anywhere you can lay out a yoga mat.

Come to your hands and knees with your wrists underneath the shoulders and your knees underneath the hips. Curl your toes under and push back through your hands to lift your hips and straighten your legs. Spread your fingers and ground down from the forearms into the fingertips.

Outwardly rotate your upper arms to broaden the collarbones. Let your head hang and move your shoulder blades away from your ears towards your hips.

Engage your quadriceps strongly to take the burden of your body's weight off your arms. This action goes a long way toward making this a resting pose. Rotate your thighs inward, keep your tail high, and sink your heels towards the floor.

Check that the distance between your hands and feet is correct by coming forward to a plank position. The distance between the hands and feet should be the same in these two poses. Do not step the feet toward the

hands in Down Dog in order the get the heels to the floor. Exhale and bend your knees to release and come back to your hands and knees.

Mindful Focusing Meditation:

This practice will help you connect with the power of choice in the present moment:

Set the Scene: Find a quiet and comfortable place to sit or lie down. Ensure you won't be disturbed during your meditation. Close your eyes or keep them gently focused on a spot in front of you.

Centering Breath: Start by taking a few deep breaths to center yourself. Inhale deeply through your nose, filling your lungs, and exhale slowly through your mouth, releasing any tension. Feel yourself becoming present.

Body Awareness: Shift your attention to your body. Notice any physical sensations, tension, or areas of discomfort. Without judgment, simply observe how your body feels in this moment.

Grounding Visualization: Imagine roots extending from the soles of your feet, anchoring you to the earth. Feel a sense of stability and grounding as you connect with the present moment.

Awareness of Thoughts: Observe your thoughts as they come and go. Recognize that you have the power to choose which thoughts to engage with and which to let pass like clouds in the sky.

Empowerment Mantra: Repeat the following mantra silently or out loud: "I am not limited by circumstances; I am empowered by the choices I make." Let these words resonate within you.

Mindful Breathing: Bring your attention to your breath. Notice the sensation of each inhale and exhale. Your breath is a reminder that you have a choice in every moment.

Choice Reflection: Think about a situation in your life where you've felt limited by circumstances. It could be a recent event or a recurring pattern. Visualize this situation without judgment.

Exploring Possibilities: As you continue to breathe mindfully, explore different choices you can make within this situation. Imagine various paths and outcomes that are open to you, even if they seem unconventional.

Letting Go of Limitations: Visualize cutting away any mental or emotional limitations that have held you back in this situation. See these limitations dissolving, leaving you feeling free and empowered.

Choosing Empowerment: Make a conscious choice to take control of the situation. Envision yourself confidently making a decision that aligns with your values and desires. Feel the empowerment that comes with this choice.

Savor the Moment: Spend a few moments basking in the feeling of empowerment and choice. Let it fill you with confidence and positivity.

Gratitude: Take a moment to express gratitude for the power of choice in your life. Recognize that, at any moment, you can choose your response to circumstances.

Return to the Breath: Shift your focus back to your breath. Breathe in strength and clarity and exhale any remaining doubts or limitations.

Closing: When you're ready to conclude the meditation, take a few deep breaths. Gently move your fingers and toes. Open your eyes if they were closed. Carry this sense of empowerment and choice into your daily life.

This mindful meditation practice reminds you that you have the power to find choice in the present moment, regardless of circumstances. By recognizing your ability to make empowering choices, you can navigate life with confidence and resilience.

SPEAK OUT

DAWN NICKEL

Founder of SHE RECOVERS® Foundation, Dawn is an accomplished thought leader in the women's recovery sphere as well as a dedicated researcher and visionary in the recovery movement. She holds a Ph.D. in health care policy with extensive experience in researching and writing about women experiencing substance use disorders, mental health challenges, and intimate partner violence.

Dawn started her own journey of recovery from a substance use disorder and domestic violence in 1987. She is also in recovery from anxiety, grief, trauma, overworking, and cancer.

RECOVERING OUT LOUD
By
Dawn Nickel

I am my best work - a series of road maps, reports, recipes, doodles, and prayers from the front lines.

—Audre Lorde

I probably was first addicted to substances by the time I was seventeen. I knew even then that I didn't think a life dominated by using was for me, but I didn't know that there was another way. I didn't think I could go completely substance free, and I just was too addicted to really moderate my use successfully. I am in recovery from substance use disorder, trauma, mental health issues (almost always anxiety but peppered with depression), and intimate partner violence.

I haven't really shared a lot about the abuse because I've always thought I had good reasons for being quiet. It was a long time ago (the mid-1980s). My ex-husband (my abuser) is still in our daughters' lives, and I hesitate to remind them of who he was and what he did to me. I was his only target; he was never, ever abusive to either of the girls.

Lately, I've been feeling like it's time I started recovering out loud about this part of my life, especially after watching the Netflix series, Maid.

So here we go.

He was the younger brother of a friend of mine, kind of cute and a little bit charming. He liked cocaine as much as I did, and because his primary occupation at the time was dealing the addictive white powder, we seemed rather perfectly matched. I was a solo mom with a three-year-old daughter and had been trying to moderate my drug and alcohol consumption since before her birth. I had experienced intermittent success with the latter. In retrospect, the main attraction to this man was that he was very kind to my sweet little girl, whose own father was not in her life. She adored him right off the bat, and I loved watching their relationship bloom. He was gentle, patient, and kind with my daughter, always.

When the abuse started after we had been together for about six months, I couldn't reconcile the two sides of him. I know now that mental abuse and violence towards inanimate objects are often precursors to physical violence. In our relationship, the first signs of trouble were when he would exhibit wordless, seething anger towards me but never explain what he was angry about. That was a total mind-bender. One evening, we were out at a bar and both of us had quite a bit to drink. Towards the end of the evening, he started giving me glaring, deadly looks. When I asked him what was wrong, he refused to tell me. Shortly after he disappeared without a word and about an hour later, I left and went home on my own.

When I arrived at our house, he was passed out in bed but the wall in the living room had a hole through it at about eye level and another at foot level, and a wicker trunk that I had treasured for years was kicked to shreds. I remember being paralyzed with fear and confusion but all I could do in the moment was grab a blanket and fall asleep on the couch.

The next morning, I asked him what happened. He told me that he had no idea and acted similarly upset at the damage in our living room. He explained that he knew he had drunk too much and taken a cab home, paid the babysitter, and went straight to bed. His explanation was that we must have had a break-in and he expressed relief that neither he nor my daughter had been harmed. The unfathomable part of domestic violence is that I believed him. The alternative – that he would have been so out of control – was too frightening for me to comprehend. Life went on for a few more months.

I want to say that drugs and alcohol were always in his system when he raged. When sober, he could be moody and sullen, but he only really lost control of himself when he was drinking and the worst he ever got was when he was doing cocaine.

Cocaine is Violence-Inducing

The first time he was physically violent towards me was when he thought I was flirting with an old friend at a wedding. I wasn't. When he started acting out at the wedding, first with the looks and then a few comments, I told him to go home and straighten out. Pregnant with my second daughter, I was stone-cold sober, and I wasn't in the mood for his nonsense. He left. When I arrived home, sober and nervous, he was sitting at the kitchen table doing lines of coke. I checked on my toddler and went to bed; he decided that I needed to admit that I had been coming on to our friend at the wedding. With every denial of mine, his anger escalated but, for some reason, he knew better than to yell and wake the three-year-old. I got out of bed to get away from him and he followed me into the kitchen.

The only place I could go to get away from him was the basement and as I opened the basement door, he shoved me. Miraculously, I didn't fall too hard because I managed to grab onto the handrail. I can still remember thinking that I couldn't fall because I was five months pregnant. I also remember being stunned that he had tried to hurl me down the stairs.

That was the time that I learned about the honeymoon period that follows most early intimate partner violence episodes. Following this episode, he was extremely remorseful. He promised to stop drinking and doing cocaine, and never accuse me, yell at me, or shove me again.

As with most victims of intimate partner violence, I believed him because I really, really wanted to believe him. As with most honeymoon periods, he couldn't do enough for me to make up for his bad behavior. Life settled and some months later we welcomed a second, beautiful daughter. We got married when she was three weeks old. He hadn't done cocaine since the stairs incident but started dealing and using it again just in time for our wedding. Still, life was calm for the most part.

Until it wasn't.

When the baby was about six months old, we had to move, and it was a really stressful time. I could not tell you what precipitated the next bout of violence, but predictably – it was worse than the previous. My only recollection was that he had been on a cocaine bender and was once again raging against me. I remember being tripped and thrown to the floor, and then trying to shield my head from his kicks while my four-year old watched and our sweet baby cried from her infant seat. He stopped after just a few minutes and fled the house. My arms and hands had shielded my head relatively well, but a few blows had landed. I did end up with a wicked headache.

And still, I didn't leave.

The next and last time I was physically assaulted by my husband was when my baby was eighteen months old. By then, I had stopped living in fear and was emboldened by the year that had passed without a violent episode. Again, details are fuzzy about what led up to the assault, but we were exchanging words and viewpoints about something that we disagreed upon. I was sitting on our living room couch holding the baby and noticing that he was ramping up with anger. For some reason, I didn't stop challenging him and he flew across the room toward me and punched me in the forehead so hard that my head ricocheted off the wall behind me.

That time I left. For a month.

Several months later, our marriage in tatters and his cocaine addiction full blown, he threatened to hit me. As in, he said the words "you better get out because I feel like I'm going to hit you again." I took my two daughters and went to the local women's shelter. It was there that an insightful counselor, after taking down my history said to me, "You have to leave. And as long as you keep using substances, you will lack the strength and follow through to leave."

By this time, I had a new resolve. I wanted to leave. I wanted to protect my kids from the insanity that I was living. I couldn't keep up with the cycle anymore:

Violence.

Honeymoon.

Calm.

Tension Building.

Violence.

Rinse and repeat.

I couldn't be the mother I needed to be in that marriage and at my deepest level, I knew that I and my daughters deserved more. It took me several more months and my husband having a psychotic break from cocaine misuse, but I did finally do what I needed to do to leave. My first step was to check in for residential treatment for my own substance use disorder. Before I left treatment, I called my husband and said that unless he stopped using all substances and got treatment for his rage, that I was coming home to get the girls and leaving for good. He said he didn't need help. I kept my word and left him. For good.

I have not drunk alcohol or done cocaine since I left that treatment program in August 1987. However, I did smoke a lot of pot for the first two years of my recovery. I have done a lot of therapy around the abuse, and I feel healed from it for the most part. In my early recovery I wrote a list of what I wanted in a relationship and a list of what I would not accept in a relationship. No rage, no name-calling, not a hint of physical aggression. I would have put "no gaslighting" on the list if that term was around at the time.

I'm fortunate. When I was ready for another relationship, I found someone who meets all of my relationship criteria. It doesn't hurt that he is also in long-term recovery. I'm grateful and I'll probably write about him another time because he is all the things I needed in a relationship that I never knew I needed.

Recovering out loud – in detail – about my past relative to intimate partner violence is new to me. But I am also realizing how important it is to me. And so here I am, hoping that some of what I write is helpful to someone else. I'll keep writing about it. There is a lot of stigma attached to this sort of violence and I want to help smash that stigma.

If you are experiencing intimate partner violence, there are people and organizations ready to support and guide you. **We do recover from the trauma of intimate partner violence.** It's not easy, but it's possible.

Help Her
RECOVER

Grounding yourself in the present
moment is like finding a steady anchor
in the storm of life.
It's a powerful tool for recovery.

~ *Jennifer Aniston*

Help Her RECOVER

By Amanda Willett

GROUNDING Principle 8, "MY BODY IS A SOURCE FOR CONNECTION, GUIDANCE, AND COPING," underscores the importance of reconnecting with one's body as a central element of recovery from gender-based violence. Survivors often endure physical and emotional disconnection during traumatic experiences. This principle encourages survivors to establish a new, healthier relationship with their bodies. By learning to listen to bodily sensations, they can better understand their needs, triggers, and boundaries. This newfound connection serves as a source of guidance, helping survivors make choices that prioritize their well-being. Additionally, grounding techniques and mindful practices allow survivors to cope with the aftermath of trauma, promoting a sense of safety and stability. Reclaiming the body as a valuable ally in the recovery journey empowers survivors to rebuild trust in themselves and establish a profound sense of self-awareness and resilience.

Dawn Nickel, Founder of SHE RECOVERS Foundation, courageously shares her personal journey of survival and recovery from gender-based violence, addiction, and trauma. She begins by reflecting on her early struggles with substance use, recognizing that her life was dominated by addiction from a young age. Despite her desire for change, she believed she couldn't achieve complete sobriety and moderation was challenging.

Dawn's story is marked by her experiences with intimate partner violence at the hands of her ex-husband. She initially kept this abuse hidden, fearing the consequences of revealing it, especially for her daughters who still had contact with their father. However, inspired by her own healing journey and the Netflix series "Maid," Dawn decides it's time to speak out and help others by sharing her story.

She delves into her relationship with her abuser, who, despite his charming facade, was deeply entwined with addiction. Dawn was drawn to him because of his kindness towards her daughter, creating a complex web of emotions. The signs of trouble began with unexplained anger and escalated to verbal and physical abuse. Dawn vividly

describes a particularly disturbing incident at a wedding, where her sobriety clashed with his cocaine-induced paranoia.

Throughout her narrative, Dawn emphasizes the link between substance abuse and violence, noting that cocaine exacerbated her abuser's aggression. She recounts incidents of violence, including physical assaults, and the subsequent "honeymoon" phases characterized by remorse and promises of change, which are common in abusive relationships.

Despite enduring horrifying episodes, Dawn remained in the relationship, driven by fear and a desperate hope for change. It wasn't until she received support from a women's shelter and an insightful counselor that she found the strength to leave her abuser. She reflects on her journey towards recovery from addiction and healing from the trauma of intimate partner violence, highlighting the importance of making a list of non-negotiables for future relationships.

Dawn's story is one of resilience, growth, and ultimately breaking free from the cycle of violence and addiction. She shares her path to recovery, which involved seeking help for her substance use disorder, ultimately leading to her ability to leave her abuser for good. Dawn ends with a message of hope, assuring others that it is possible to recover from intimate partner violence and encouraging survivors to seek support.

In this chapter, Dawn Nickel embodies the GROUNDING Principle 8, "MY BODY IS A SOURCE FOR CONNECTION, GUIDANCE, AND COPING," by illustrating her journey of reconnecting with herself, finding strength in her body, and using it as a vessel for transformation and healing. Her story serves as a beacon of hope and an inspiration for others who may be experiencing similar challenges, reminding them that recover is possible and they are not alone.

GROUNDING

Principle 8:
MY BODY IS A SOURCE FOR CONNECTION, GUIDANCE, AND COPING

Reflect on your current connection with your body. How often do you consciously check in with your physical sensations and how they relate to your overall well-being?

Rituals for Recovery

Affirmation:

I am a constant source of guidance, reminding me to stay present and aligned with my true self.

Savasana

Getting into Savasana is inviting both your mind and body into a calm space but can be more challenging than it first appears.

Starting on your back, take your feet as wide as your mat and allow your feet to fall open. Turn your palms up and place your arms at your sides. Close your eyes, breathe in deeply through your nose, and exhale with a deep sigh through your mouth. Allow your entire body to relax and be present.

Mindful Focusing Meditation:

This practice will help you connect with your body's wisdom and presence:

1. **Find a Quiet Space:** Choose a quiet and comfortable space where you won't be disturbed. Sit in a comfortable position with your spine straight, or you can also lie down if that's more comfortable for you.

2. **Close Your Eyes:** Close your eyes gently to minimize external distractions and turn your attention inward.
3. **Take Centering Breaths:** Begin by taking a few deep breaths. Inhale deeply through your nose, allowing your abdomen to rise, and exhale slowly through your mouth, releasing any tension. Do these three to five times.
4. **Body Scan:** Shift your focus to your body. Start at the top of your head and slowly move your attention down through your body, paying close attention to each part. Notice any areas of tension, discomfort, or sensation.
5. **Tune into Sensations:** As you scan your body, become fully aware of the sensations you're experiencing. It might be warmth, coolness, tingling, or any other feeling. Acknowledge these sensations without judgment.
6. **Breathing into Sensations:** When you encounter areas of tension or discomfort, take a deep breath and direct your breath to that specific area. Imagine your breath as a warm, soothing light that flows to the tense area, bringing relaxation and comfort.
7. **Connect with Your Heart:** Place your hand over your heart and take a few breaths, focusing on the rise and fall of your chest. Feel the beating of your heart, reminding you of your true essence and presence.
8. **Align with Your True Self:** Reflect on the concept of your "true self." Visualize your true self as a source of wisdom, love, and authenticity. It is the part of you that knows your deepest desires and values.
9. **Body as a Compass:** Imagine your body as a compass guiding you toward your true self. Feel the connection between your physical sensations and your inner wisdom. Trust that your body knows the way.

10. **Stay Present:** Keep your attention on your body and breath. If your mind starts to wander, gently bring it back to the sensations in your body. This practice is about staying present and connected.

11. **Inner Dialogue:** Ask yourself if there's any guidance or insight that your body is trying to convey to you in this moment. It might be a subtle feeling or intuition. Be open to any messages that arise.

12. **Gratitude:** Express gratitude to your body for its constant guidance and wisdom. Acknowledge that it is always with you, supporting you on your journey.

13. **Closing:** When you're ready to conclude the meditation, take a few more deep breaths. Gently wiggle your fingers and toes. Open your eyes if they were closed. Carry the sense of alignment and connection with your true self into your day.

This meditation practice helps you recognize that your body is a constant source of guidance and wisdom. By staying present and tuning into your body's sensations, you can align yourself with your true self, making choices and decisions that resonate with your deepest values and desires.

SPEAK OUT

AUDREY MONETTE

Audrey works for a national crime prevention organization and leads diverse projects related to community safety and well-being (CSWB), including facilitating training sessions, conducting research, and developing CSWB plans. With a master's degree in critical criminology, she advocates for non-carceral approaches to ending gender-based violence, preventing victimization, and improving victims' and prisoners' rights.

Audrey is passionate about community-led approaches to safety and well-being that are rooted in equity, social justice, and dismantling systems of oppression. She lives in Gatineau, Québec with her partner of twelve years and her bunny.

I WAS ONLY FIFTEEN: A JOURNEY TO SURVIVING DOMESTIC VIOLENCE AS A TEENAGER

By
Audrey Monette

I am not free while any woman is unfree, even when her shackles are very different from my own.

—Audre Lorde

I was 15 years old when I became a survivor. Like most teenagers at that time, I didn't know much about domestic violence. It was a distant concept I never believed could find a place within the borders of my own life.

My story differs from those I had heard about; talking about my experience felt unjustifiable, like a drop in the ocean of the thousands of women I believed had it worse. I made myself believe that my young age and our absence of cohabitation and children somehow diminished its significance, making my experience less meaningful than others. I now know differently. Experiencing domestic violence during adolescence is detrimental for survivors' development, health, self-esteem, and sense of safety. Years later, when I could finally understand the impact of domestic violence, when I could see its far-reaching impacts and how it fundamentally changes someone, I finally found my voice and the courage to add my own drop in the ocean. Domestic violence does not only impact older or more established couples—youth and young adults are not immune to the experience. If I had been more aware of the different forms of violence, perhaps I would have been better equipped to detect those behaviours. Perhaps I would have been able to escape a situation that caused me irreparable harm. To prevent intimate partner violence in all its forms, we must talk about it to reduce the stigma. And we must do more to educate young people.

I was only fifteen years old. He was over eighteen years old. Power dynamics were severely unbalanced, which considerably exacerbated the violence within our relationship. While various forms of violence occurred *during* the relationship, they continued to escalate *after* the relationship ended. Sometimes, separation is not always a guarantee of safety for victims of intimate partner violence because the partner who caused harm wants to continue to exert control, seek revenge, or convince the person to return. Post-separation violence is common in cases of domestic violence, but it tends to be overlooked.

> According to Women and Gender Equality Canada (2022), "intimate partner violence (IPV), also known as spousal or domestic violence, is a prevalent form of gender-based violence (GBV). It refers to multiple forms of harm caused by a current or former intimate partner or spouse." IPV can occur in both public and private spaces, as well as online, and can include:
>
> - **physical abuse:** intentional or threatened use of physical force, including pushing, hitting, shoving
> - **criminal harassment (also referred to as stalking)**: repeated conduct that creates fear for one's safety or the safety of a loved one. The repeated conduct can include

> making threats, obscene phone calls, following, watching, tracking, contacting on the Internet, including through texts or email messages
>
> - **sexual violence:** sexual acts without consent, threats of repercussions for refusing sexual activity, forcing someone to watch or participate in the making of pornography, sexually degrading language and belittling sexual comments
>
> - **emotional /psychological abuse:** insults, belittling, constant humiliation, intimidation, threats of harm, threats to take away children, harm or threat of harm to pets
>
> - **financial abuse (also referred to as economic abuse):** control or misuse of money, assets or property, control of a partner's ability to access school or a job
>
> Source: https://women-gender-equality.canada.ca/en/gender-based-violence/intimate-partner-violence.html

I was born in 1994 and grew up in a military family. My father's career in the Canadian Armed Forces led us to move throughout the country every few years. Despite the frequent moves, one thing remained constant: my parents' loving relationship and the positive environment they fostered in our home. I was always aware of how privileged my younger brother and I were to grow up in a supportive and caring household. I promised myself to emulate that in my own relationship someday.

In July 2007, my father was posted to Québec City. We had spent the previous four years living in Borden, Ontario, which was a particularly challenging time for me. I was in middle school and was heavily bullied by my classmates, which had devastating impacts on my mental health, well-being, and self-esteem. My mind spiralled with thoughts of suicide, giving in to self-harming behaviour. When we finally moved to Québec City, I was thrilled to start anew, but unbeknownst to me, a new set of challenges was awaiting. Because the school system is different in the province of Québec, my peers of the same age were already in high school and manifested a greater level of maturity than me – they were interested in dating, drinking, and other activities that I had never considered as a thirteen-year-old. At this point, I had never received any education on dating, relationships, consent, contraception, or sexual health. Nevertheless, I quickly made friends and adapted to the culture and activities in Québec City. I dated a few boys, but none of those relationships were serious.

When I turned fifteen, with my parents' permission, I got my first job in a restaurant a couple of streets away from our house. During the school year, I worked a few weeknights and weekends, and I extended my hours during the summer break, gaining my first real feeling of independence. My parents bought a motor scooter which they allowed me to use to drive to work by myself. A few weeks after starting the job, I was leaving work on my scooter when I suddenly got hit by a car that didn't see me pulling out of the exit. In shock, I ignored the sharp pain in my leg and the blood on my hands. I stood up and let out a sigh of relief when I realized the scooter only had a few scratches – I desperately wanted to drive home. Fortunately, a co-worker of mine happened to be outside during his break when the accident occurred. He hurried over to me and made sure I was unharmed before helping me climb back onto my scooter. I cried all the way home.

Following the accident, my co-worker and I found ourselves drawn to each other, our conversations growing more frequent during our shared shifts. A few weeks later, he invited me on a date. We started spending a significant amount of time together and within a month, we were officially in a relationship. It was my first real relationship. He was an adult—nineteen years old—and I was fifteen.

> According to the 2018 Survey of Safety in Public and Private Spaces, more than four in ten (44%) women—who had ever been in an intimate partner relationship—reported experiencing some form of IPV in their lifetime (since age 15). Looking specifically at young women aged 15 to 24 years, almost three in ten (29%) reported experiencing some form of IPV in the 12 months preceding the survey. This proportion was much higher than that observed among ever-partnered women aged 25 years and older (10%). In the 12 months preceding the survey, young women were more likely than women aged 25 years and older to experience all three categories of IPV measured by the survey.
>
> Source: https://women-gender-equality.canada.ca/en/gender-based-violence/intimate-partner-violence.html

Given the age gap between us, our lifestyles were drastically different. His friend group was older, he was allowed to drink and go to bars, and we did not share the same hobbies or interests. Despite this, the first two months of the relationship were joyful. He lived with his parents, so I quickly met his family, spent a lot of time at their home, and we continued to work together at the restaurant. However, he refused to meet my parents and friends and he never wanted us to spend time at my house. While I did not perceive this as an issue in the beginning, my parents quickly started to disapprove of the relationship. For them, the age gap was a concern, and his lack of interest in meeting my loved ones was a real preoccupation. In hindsight, I know my parents only wanted to protect me as any parent would, but at the time, it had the opposite effect – I isolated myself more. Looking back, I am convinced that my reaction was not a coincidence. My partner's behaviour directly fostered and encouraged isolation. In fact, his refusal to meet my parents and his resistance to spending time with my friends were a deliberate effort to isolate me from my support system.

> Social isolation is a common type of abuse in situations of intimate partner violence. Social isolation is behaviour that aims to cut the victim from their family, friends, or community. It can also involve behaviours to damage the victim's relationship with others. Social isolation abuse can include various behaviours including stopping the victim from seeing friends, family, or other people; not allowing the victim to leave their home or participate in social activities; needing to know where the victim is or who they are planning to see; and more (DV Connect, 2020).
>
> Source: https://www.dvconnect.org/social-isolation-can-be-domestic-violence/

In addition to isolating me from my family, he denigrated my friends, preventing me from spending time with them and accusing them of being too immature and boring. If I had plans with my friends, he often made me feel guilty or got angry at me for choosing them over him. This contributed to me falling deeper into isolation, as I sought to escape his anger and the embarrassment it brought. We rarely spent time in public together outside of our work shifts at the restaurant. I felt like he was ashamed of being seen with me. In fact, he had a habit of commenting on my physical appearance and persistently trying to exert control over how I looked and dressed. If I wore leggings or did my makeup, he accused me of seeking attention and wanting to attract other men. If I wore jeans and didn't wear makeup, he would criticize me for not taking proper care of myself and would state that he was ashamed of me. There was no winning. We spent most of our time alone in the basement of his parents' house. Despite this, I thought he loved me. And I loved him.

Four months into the relationship, things took a turn for the worse. He became more aggressive and more violent. At that time, I was not aware of the various types of intimate partner violence—a lot of which had already been occurring. It became increasingly clear to me, however, that something was wrong. First, the psychological violence increased drastically. He continued to comment on my appearance, but also started to make degrading comments about my intelligence and worthiness. He repeatedly asserted that without him, I would amount to nothing and that I would never find another man willing to be with me. He also began to flirt with other women in front of me, including our co-workers. He frequently discussed other women, telling me that they were more beautiful, smart, and mature than me. My self-confidence was severely impacted by these incessant comments. I still carry many of those insecurities with me today.

At this point in the relationship, he also began disappearing for extended periods, days on end, during which he would sever all lines of communication with me. He often left his home and turned off his phone for three to four days at a time. Obviously, I became extremely worried and when I contacted his parents and friends to ask where he was, they all covered for him and told me they did not know. When he reappeared several days later, upon discovering that I had reached out to his loved ones or noticing my missed calls and messages, his response was anger and he often told me that he did not owe me anything. I was told that I was jealous, "crazy", and insecure. To this day, I do not know where he went during those frequent absences.

In addition to the ongoing psychological violence, he started displaying physically violent behaviour. It was my first serious relationship, so I had virtually no prior sexual experience and very little knowledge about safe sexual practices. Throughout the relationship, he often forced me to have sex when I didn't want to and guilted me into trying sexual practices that I was not comfortable with. If I refused intimacy, he got angry. Very angry. He once punched a hole in the wall next to my head while I was laying in bed. Frequently, he resorted to pushing and shoving, though since he never hit me directly, I did not realize I was experiencing abuse. I was still constantly afraid for my safety, so I learned to stop saying no. I was sexually assaulted repeatedly by this person who was supposed to love me. Eventually, instances of non-consensual sex led to injuries, some of which persist to this day.

One night, I was seriously injured after non-consensual sexual intercourse. When he realized what he had done, he ran away. He got dressed, grabbed his keys, and fled. He left me alone in his room, covered in blood. I will always remember seeing his car back out of the driveway through the small basement window. His mother, who was upstairs, heard me crying and rushed to help me. She helped me clean up, get dressed, and drove me home. My parents were away at a hockey tournament with my younger brother that weekend. I cried, alone, as I washed the blood off my clothes. I scrubbed so hard that I woke up with blisters on my fingers the next day.

A few days after this incident, I found myself back at his place. His mother was outside smoking a cigarette and invited me to join her. I sat with her, and we talked for several hours. She told me that I should leave before it's too late. I couldn't find it within me to walk away.

> The reasons why women stay in a violent relationship are diverse and complex. The most dangerous time for a survivor of intimate partner violence in when they attempt to leave an abusive partner. According to the Canadian Women's Foundation (2022), "the mental health consequences of abuse can make it even more difficult to leave. Abusive relationships can develop in a gradual process where violence escalates over time. The experience can harm mental health and self-confidence, instill fear, and make it difficult for to believe a safer future is even possible". Source: https://canadianwomen.org/the-facts/gender-based-violence/

One year into the relationship, after disappearing for several days again, he finally called me. Relieved, I picked up the phone. Before I could say anything, he told me he no longer loved me and that he was breaking up with me. I immediately felt shocked, broken, and inadequate. Just like that, our relationship was over. But the story does not end here. In fact, it gets worse. The violence did not stop, it just transitioned to a new form of abuse – post separation violence.

After breaking up, my ex-partner and I still worked together, although our schedules rarely overlapped since I was also in school. A few weeks after the separation, I reconnected with an old friend of mine, Sam, who I hadn't been in touch with for a few years. We started chatting online and spending time together, and he immediately made me feel safe and seen. Sam was kind, gentle, and understanding. Soon, we made our relationship official (spoiler alert – this friend is now my partner of thirteen years!). I was happier than ever.

A month into our relationship, Sam was celebrating his 17th birthday, so one night after school I stopped by the mall to buy him a birthday present—a brand-new GPS for his car. I was working that night, so I took the bus from the mall and went directly to work. When I walked into the back door of the restaurant, I froze. My ex-partner was there, filling in for someone else's shift. He immediately noticed the GPS in my hands and asked who it was for. My hesitation made it obvious that I didn't want to tell him, so he figured I must be seeing someone else. I remember the expression on his face changing and I could tell he was angry. I was terrified. That night, he whispered derogatory and threatening comments to me each time I walked past in him in the restaurant. He shoved me against walls, ran into me intentionally, and deliberately tried to intimidate me with his words and actions.

A few weeks later, Sam and I planned a movie night, so we walked from my parents' house to the movie rental store. On the way back we decided to stop by the restaurant where I worked to grab a snack and seek refuge from the cold. My ex-partner usually didn't work evening shifts, so I wasn't worried. As we entered, my heart sank upon spotting him in the kitchen. The moment he noticed us, he connected the dots and realized this was the new person I was seeing. He immediately pointed to the back door, wanting me to meet him there. With a heart pounding in fear, I made my way to the back door. He yelled at me, called me names, insulted my new boyfriend, and threatened me. I tried to mask the turmoil as I returned to the table where Sam was sitting, but I had lost my appetite. That night, Sam sensed that something was wrong and gently encouraged me to share what had occurred. I immediately broke down. I told him everything that I experienced in my previous relationship – the derogatory comments, the isolation, the control, the injuries, the violence, and the trauma I was still dealing with. Unsurprisingly, he was devastated but remained understanding and empathetic.

Little did I know, my ex-partner was even more furious than I imagined. In the following weeks, my boyfriend drove me to work a few times, and my ex figured out which car he drove. One night, Sam slept over at my parents' house with me, so his car was parked on the street. When we woke up the next morning, we realized that someone had shot paintballs at his car and smashed a window. While we didn't know for sure that my ex had done it, my boyfriend, my parents, and I shared the suspicion that it was him. A few days later, my boyfriend woke up at his house and someone had broken into the car and stole the GPS I bought him for his birthday. The GPS cord had been cut and left behind, making it impossible to use the device or sell it for profit. The person who stole it simply wanted to cause harm. Again, we suspected that my ex-partner was responsible. This situation was particularly alarming because it happened at my boyfriend's residence, implying that my ex must have been following him to discover where he lived.

The following months were exhausting. I still worked at the same restaurant, so my ex and I sometimes had overlapping shifts. When we worked together, he continued to harass and bully me. Once, I was in the commercial fridge in the back of the restaurant and he shut the door behind me, turned the light off, and blocked the door so I couldn't escape. I was locked in the fridge for several minutes before another employee walked in and found me, confused. In order to cross from the front to the rear of the restaurant, I had to walk down a narrow corridor adjacent to the kitchen. Bordering the hallway was a large commercial hotdog steamer. On multiple occasions, he grabbed my arm as I passed and held it against the steamer to burn me. I vividly remember crying at night, running my fingers against the burn scars on my arms. Eventually, I told the restaurant owner what was going on. Her response was incredibly supportive, and she immediately reorganized the work schedule to ensure I would no longer have to work alongside my ex. From there, the situation began to improve.

That summer, my parents and brother planned a trip to the United States. I stayed home because I was working full-time at the restaurant during the summer break. I was excited to spend two weeks alone at home, and I asked my parents if I could invite some friends over while they were away. With their permission, I invited a few of my co-workers to have a bonfire in my backyard after work one night. Some of my co-workers were also friends with my ex-partner, but most of them were not aware of the situation between him and I. Unfortunately, one of my co-workers mentioned to my ex that I had invited some friends over to my house since my parents were away on vacation. Although my ex was not surprised that he was not invited, he did retain one crucial piece of information—my parents were away for two weeks. I was home alone.

During those weeks, he started driving around my neighbourhood and parking his car in front my house to scare me. There was a door at the back of the house that provided direct access to the basement, where my room was located. The back door had a lockbox which allowed to access the key by inputting a code. Given our history, my ex knew the code to the lockbox. One night, I heard him unlock the door and break into the house. I pretended to sleep but could see his reflection in the small television next to my bed. He stood in the basement, stared at me for a few minutes, and left. I didn't want to tell my parents because I knew they would be worried and would want to come home from their vacation, so I stayed awake and held my breath every night until they got back.

At the end of the summer, he left his job at the restaurant, and I learned that he had met someone new. I remember feeling relieved that I would no longer see him at work and hoped he would shift his focus away from me now that he was in a relationship. Despite this, I was worried that his new partner would experience the same violence I had endured. Soon, I stopped hearing from him, but I continued to be hypervigilant and was terrified of running into him every time I left my house. Luckily, I never did.

I eventually began to feel less anxious and was slowly starting to heal. I was still in a safe and healthy relationship with Sam and was working on building back my self-esteem and confidence. One afternoon, I received a message on Facebook from a woman I didn't know. I clicked to read it and my heart sank as soon as I read the first sentence – it was a message from his current girlfriend. She told me she was stuck in an abusive relationship and asked me if I had experienced the same thing. She described everything he did—psychological, sexual, and physical violence. I was devastated. We messaged back and forth for hours, sharing our respective stories and trying to offer each other solace and support.

I did not expect what happened next. The following day, I came home from school and was doing homework with Sam and a friend when I got a call from an unknown number. I picked up and panicked when I heard my ex's voice telling me he caught his girlfriend messaging me the day before. He began screaming and threatening me over the phone, accusing me of trying to sabotage his relationship. The situation escalated in the following hours – he called and texted me hundreds of times, sending me extremely serious threats. My boyfriend, my friend, and I alerted my parents of the situation because we were concerned for my safety. My parents asked me to go spend the night at Sam's house in case my ex tried to show up at my house to hurt me.

I woke up with hundreds of missed calls and text messages the following day. He threatened my family, my friends, my boyfriend, and my dog. He left dozens of voicemails with threatening messages, in which he detailed his intentions to physically harm me, even going so far as to threaten to beat me up and disfigure me by running me over with his car. He also managed to find my school schedule and sent messages claiming that he hired women to follow me to class and beat me up. My parents and boyfriend advised me to start taking random buses after school, getting off at different stops, and calling them to come pick me up so these women could not follow me home. I alerted the security agents at school and never walked alone in public. In the following weeks, my ex began to drive around my neighbourhood and park in front of my house again. My mental health deteriorated, my grades plummeted, and I was unable to sleep for several weeks. My parents eventually made the decision to call his parents, hoping to shed light on their son's behaviour. His parents dismissed the situation. They refused to help.

After several weeks, my parents and I decided to report the situation to the police; we were increasingly afraid for our safety. I took screenshots of all the text messages and call logs on my phone and uploaded them to my computer. It was incredibly traumatizing to read the messages every time I opened my phone, so I deleted all the original messages after saving the screenshots to my computer. My mother contacted a friend who was a police officer, seeking guidance on the steps required to report the situation.

When I told the police officer that I had saved screenshots of the messages and deleted them from my phone, she told me they would not be receivable in court since the original files were no longer available. Therefore, if we were to go to court, it would be my word against his. The police officer also told us that domestic violence is particularly difficult to prove in court, and that the process would be long, difficult, and traumatizing. She deterred me from filing an official report, so I didn't.

> According to the 2021 GSS on Victimization, the large majority (80%) of victims of intimate partner violence do not report the violence they experience to police. Among those who did report to police, only one-third (32%) of victims reported that police laid charges against their spouse.
>
> Source: https://www150.statcan.gc.ca/n1/pub/85-002-x/2021001/article/00014-eng.htm

During this period, I changed my phone number, blocked my ex-partner from all social media platforms, and changed the code to the door of my house. I eventually quit my job at the restaurant and started working somewhere else so he would not be aware of my workplace. He stopped calling and texting me, and the fear slowly started to dissipate. I continued to be afraid of running into him in public spaces. Luckily, I never did. Again, I slowly started to heal.

The trauma from surviving intimate partner violence, particularly at such a key developmental stage, was severe. I felt ashamed, guilty, and confused about my experience. I was angry at myself for staying in the relationship for as long as I did, and I had endless questions about the factors that lead someone to commit domestic violence. Soon, it was time for me to apply to university. Up to this point, I wanted to become a translator, but I decided to apply for an undergraduate program in criminology instead. My decision to study criminology was directly influenced by my experience of surviving intimate partner violence. I felt like it would help me feel empowered by better understanding my experience, including the causes and the impacts. My criminology courses helped me recognize the different types of violence I had experienced beyond physical violence. They also helped me make sense of my experience, which in turn reduced my fear, shame, and anger. This knowledge was an integral part of my recovery journey.

My healing process also included implementing several tangible actions to increase my physical safety. For instance, I changed my phone number, changed my door locks, and got a new job. It felt empowering to put these concrete measures into place because it felt like I was reclaiming control over my environment and space, while also reducing opportunities for my ex-partner to find me, to contact me, and – ultimately – to harm me.

My support system continues to be a key part of my recovery. My boyfriend, my family, and my friends who listened to me, believed me, and looked out for me during those years allowed me to rest and heal. Their empathy and love provided a safe space for me to go once I felt ready to speak out about my experience. In addition to informal supports, seeking professional support and therapy also contributed to my recovery. While professional help is not accessible to everyone due to financial and systemic barriers that remain a key issue for victims of gender-based violence, it can be an integral tool to support journeys of healing and recovery. My therapist allowed me to deconstruct some of the perceptions, beliefs, and behaviours I displayed that were rooted in my experience of intimate partner violence.

My journey to recovery is far from done. Every day, I am reminded of the trauma I carry from surviving domestic violence. Even though I am in a loving, nurturing, and safe relationship, I moved hundreds of kilometers away from the city in which I lived when this story happened, and even if I graduated with a master's degree in criminology, I still deal with the physical and psychological harm from my first relationship. Recovering from intimate partner violence will be a lifelong process.

Nevertheless, my experience inspired my career in violence prevention. I now work for a national organization that helps municipalities increase community safety and prevent violence through upstream approaches rooted in social justice and social development. Through my work, I support communities in identifying the root causes of crime and violence, and effective ways to address them. This involves making criminological research accessible for decision-makers, offering training sessions and presentations, and working with communities on the development of community safety plans. I also volunteer with various feminist grassroots organizations in my community who advocate for the rights and needs of survivors of gender-based violence. I was finally able to find my voice, which I now use to advocate for non-carceral approaches to justice and for improved rights for survivors of interpersonal and systemic violence.

Every day I wake up and do this work in hopes to contribute to preventing other women and girls from experiencing intimate partner violence, but also to remind myself that I did not survive in vain. I am a survivor, and I will continue to fight so women, girls, and gender-diverse people can be safe, thrive, and never have to just survive.

Intimate partner violence is preventable:

- Teach safe and healthy relationship skills through school curricula.
- Train children and youth on emotional regulation and positive conflict resolution.
- Increase funding for bystander intervention training and education.
- Challenge social norms that foster or encourage violence.
- Prevent risk factors that can lead to IPV through parenting support programs.
- Support survivors through housing, employment, and food security initiatives.

Source: Waller, I. (2019). *Science and Secrets of Ending Violent Crime.* Rowman & Littlefield Publishers.

Help Her RECOVER

Yourself, as much as anybody in the entire universe,
deserve your love and affection.

~ *Sharon Stone*

Help Her RECOVER

By Amanda Willett

OWNERSHIP Principle 9, "I CAN CREATE THE CONDITIONS FOR SAFETY AND GROWTH," emphasizes the survivor's agency in shaping their healing journey after experiencing gender-based violence. It recognizes that survivors have the capacity to establish an environment that prioritizes their safety, growth, and well-being. This principle encourages survivors to take ownership of their recovery process by setting boundaries, seeking support, and making choices that align with their healing goals. By creating conditions conducive to healing, survivors can regain a sense of control over their lives, fostering an atmosphere where they can flourish and rebuild their self-esteem. Ultimately, this principle empowers survivors to transform their experiences of violence into a catalyst for personal growth and empowerment, allowing them to reclaim their lives with strength and resilience.

Audrey Monette shares her harrowing experience of surviving domestic violence as a teenager highlighting the importance of creating safe environments for young individuals to grow and develop. At the age of fifteen, Audrey entered a relationship with an older partner, and the significant age gap created power dynamics that exacerbated violence within the relationship. Audrey's lack of knowledge about healthy relationships and consent, along with her isolation from her support system, contributed to her vulnerability.

Her narrative underscores the critical need for education and awareness about intimate partner violence among young people. Audrey emphasizes that domestic violence is not limited to older or more established couples; it can impact youth and young adults as well. She regrets not being more aware of the signs of abuse and the various forms it can take.

Audrey's story also sheds light on the often-overlooked issue of post-separation violence, where abusers continue to exert control and harm their victims even after the relationship ends. This further emphasizes the need for creating safe conditions for survivors to escape and recover.

Throughout her journey, Audrey demonstrates resilience and courage. She shares her path of recovery, highlighting the importance of support systems, both informal and professional, in the healing process.

Her story serves as an inspiration for others who have experienced intimate partner violence, and she has turned her experience into a driving force for violence prevention and advocacy.

Audrey Monette illustrates how her experience as a survivor of domestic violence as a teenager underscores the importance of creating safe conditions for young individuals, providing education on healthy relationships, and offering support for those affected by gender-based violence. Her journey to healing and her subsequent work in violence prevention exemplify the theme of ownership as she transformed her experience of violence into fuel for personal empowerment.

OWNERSHIP

Principle 9:
I CAN CREATE THE CONDITIONS
FOR SAFETY AND GROWTH

Explore your beliefs about safety and growth.
Are there any limiting beliefs that might be hindering your ability
to create the conditions you desire?
How can you challenge and change those beliefs?

RITUALS FOR Recovery

Affirmation:

I take full ownership of my life, creating a safe and nurturing environment for my growth.

Forward Fold, Uttanasana

Stand with your heels 2–3 inches away from the wall and lean your sacrum against it. Use your inhale to lengthen through your upper body, soften your knees and then fold forward from your hip flexors on your exhale. Let your head and arms hang heavy and gently tilt your sit bones up the wall until you feel a gentle stretch in your hamstrings. You can judge for yourself how far feels comfort- able to fold forward. Allow your body to slowly ease into the pose over 5 – 10 breaths. Using your breath to support your body in the pose. When done correctly, it can help to improve posture, extend the spine, and stretch tight hamstrings. It is also an excellent pose for relieving stress, deepening mindful- ness, and calming the mind.

Mindful Focusing Meditation:

Here's a mindful meditation practice to help you embody the theme of taking ownership and creating a safe environment for your growth:

1. **Find a Quiet Space:** Begin by finding a quiet and comfort- able place to sit or lie down. Ensure that you won't be disturbed during your meditation.
2. **Relax Your Body:** Close your eyes and take a few deep breaths. Inhale deeply through your nose, and exhale slowly through your mouth. As you exhale, let go of any tension in your body.
3. **Grounding Visualization:** Imagine yourself standing in a peaceful and safe place in nature. It could be a serene forest, a calming beach, or a tranquil meadow. Feel the stability of the ground beneath your feet. This place represents your inner sanctuary, where you have complete control.
4. **Embody Ownership:** As you stand in this safe space, bring your awareness to the concept of ownership. Visualize yourself taking full ownership of your life and your surroundings. Imagine holding a symbolic key that represents your power and responsi- bility for your life.
5. **Create a Safe Bubble:** Visualize a shimmering, protective bubble form- ing around you. This bubble represents the safe and nurturing envi- ronment you are creating for yourself. It shields you from external negativity and influences.
6. **Breathe in Safety:** As you breathe in, imagine that you are inhaling safety, empowerment, and growth. Feel these qualities filling every cell of your body. Sense how they nurture and support your well- being.
7. **Exhale Negativity:** With each exhale, release any doubts, fears, or negativity that may have been holding you back. Let go of past limita- tions and external pressures. See them dissipate as you breathe out.

8. **Affirmation:** Repeat the affirmation silently or aloud: "I take full ownership of my life, creating a safe and nurturing environment for my growth." Say this affirmation with conviction, believing in your ability to create this environment.

9. **Feel the Empowerment:** Sense the empowerment and strength growing within you. Visualize your life as a canvas, and you are the artist. You have the power to shape your reality and design your path.

10. **Connect with Your Inner Wisdom:** Place your hand on your heart and take a moment to connect with your inner wisdom. Trust your intuition and the choices you make to foster safety and growth.

11. **Gratitude:** Express gratitude for this moment of self-empowerment and the ability to create your safe haven. Acknowledge your own strength and determination.

12. **Silent Reflection:** Sit in silence for a few minutes, allowing the feeling of ownership and safety to resonate within you. Embrace the sense of responsibility for your life.

13. **Closing:** When you're ready to conclude your meditation, slowly open your eyes. Carry the sense of ownership and empowerment with you as you move forward in your day.

This meditation practice helps you cultivate a deep sense of ownership over your life. By visualizing and affirming your power to create a safe and nurturing environment, you reinforce your commitment to growth and well-being. This sense of ownership can serve as a foundation for making choices that align with your goals and values.

SPEAK OUT

MARY ANNE GRONNINGEN

Mary Anne is devoted to helping elderly women create their dream lives. She was a little girl when World War II ended and her traumatized father returned. He was as good to her as he was capable, but her mother and so-called aunties punished her constantly. She was expected to relinquish her hopes and education to help her mother raise her younger brothers and sister. Mary Anne quickly learned it was easiest not to voice an opinion; she said "yes" to everything.

Her beauty led her to modeling opportunities cut short by sexual harassment. In Norway, she was assumed to be a prostitute and she had to actively protect her children from the parents of their peers. For too many years, she lived a life of fear and was embarrassed and ashamed by her past and all the secrets she was forced to carry. Only in her 70s did she break free and start to create a life of freedom for herself. Mary Anne has two children and four grandchildren. She spreads her time between her homes in Norway and Spain where she cares for her husband and their little dog, Proffen.

EMERGING FROM PAIN THROUGH LOVE AND A LIFE OF SERVICE

By
Mary Anne Gronningen

History, despite its wrenching pain, cannot be unlived, but if faced with courage, need not be lived again.

—Maya Angelou

I did not have a childhood, that period where you are supposed to be cherished and taken care of. We lived in cramped rooms with my parents and other adults, some family, some not, who punished me often. Many of these adults were ill-treated themselves as children. My mother was an orphan who I know was frequently beaten by her grandparents. She never went to school, not for even one day. So perhaps she and the other adults around did not have the patience or did not even consider that they should be kind to children. No one had been kind to them. I grew up unprotected and feeling like I was nothing.

In one of my earliest memories, it was a rough-looking man wearing only short pants who yelled at me and saved my life. I was seven years old, and my mother had sent me to rinse the diaper of her newest baby, my third brother, Michael. I was the oldest girl of seven children, so this type of work fell to me. We were very poor, and this was many decades before the time of disposable diapers. My mother made diapers by cutting a larger piece of flannel into pieces. She had very few of them, so each diaper was precious. My job was to take the soiled diapers and rinse them in the cold and pristine water that came down through drains from the hilltop, creating a pond that ran into a little rivulet. At the base of the drain, within the shallow part of the pond, were two stones to stand on. The water from the drain poured like a strong waterfall between the stones, so the drain was excellent for this task. On this day, a thin, orange, and yellowish snake startled me as it appeared in the water beneath me. I dropped the diaper, and the fast-moving, strong current carried it away.

I knew I could not go home without it–my mother would be furious. I tried to catch that diaper without straying from the rocky shore, but it moved too fast. It would come tantalizingly close, and I'd grab for it, but it would slip away. I raced along the edges of the water, focusing only on the fabric when suddenly this black-haired man was in front of me yelling at me. He grabbed my arm, pulling me up and shaking me such that I was dangling, my feet unable to touch the ground.

"Stupid girl! What are you doing? Let it go! You will drown."

I tried to get away, saying "if I do not get it back, I'll get a beating." Crying, I saw the diaper float away. I looked up at the man, but at that time, I did not think of him as having saved my life. He was just another adult yelling at me and calling me stupid. I had no option but to return home and accept my punishment.

My mother was an orphan and had come from mainland China to Malaysia for work. She never had a day of school. In Malaysia, she met my father. My father was an accountant before he volunteered to go to fight with the Australia forces in World War II. I was born soon after my father returned broken and traumatized but with three medals for his bravery. He had been captured and tortured; his body was worn out. He was tired due to all he had suffered and the journey home, plus more tired from all that he did to bring the insufficient amount of money he obtained through any job he could find. Despite being an accountant, he did not make much money because of the racism of the times. The British accountant clerks, less educated than he, got the majority of money and the privilege of discounted goods, free housing, and free maid services.

We lived in houses with many family members and others who I called aunties and uncles anyway. At one point we moved to the jungles of Singapore. We had no electricity, and I was afraid of the dark. My job was to find firewood and dried coconut leaves to create a stove for cooking. By the time I did my chores, it would be dark outside, and I would hang a kerosene lantern from a tree to do my homework. I had to cook, clean, and take care of the kids while the adults bullied me, as well as one of my brothers.

All the adults in the house—my father's friends and my mother's younger brother in particular—beat us. They would pull my ears and make me do pull ups where I had to cross my arms across my chest and grasp my ears, so I was holding my left ear with my right hand and vice-versa. My brother was made to do this too and then we were ordered to squat, going up and down. If we stopped, she would get the cane. My uncle had been a prisoner in a Japanese camp during the war and he seemed inspired by the tortures he'd learned there. He used more of them on my brother than on me, but I could do nothing to help my brother, which hurt as much as the abuse.

I never got to play. Never had a doll or toy in my hands. Never had a chance to run and do the things I saw other kids doing. Some girls I met at school would come by the house, calling out to me to come play, but my mother would not allow me to go. On a few occasions she let me run around with my sister, but as I was holding her in my arms, I could not really play.

I loved school but was not considered smart. At school, the teachers made fun of me. While most of the kids started the new school year with fresh new notebooks, a new spic-and-span uniform consisting of a green dress with a white shift underneath, shoes, and white ribbons in their hair, it would be months into the school year before my parents would scrape enough money together to get me even a notebook.

Each morning I had to make my father tea at six am followed by a whole list of chores which made it impossible to get to school on time. School was a twenty-minute walk away and I never had money for buses. As much as I tried to get to school on time, I couldn't and was cruelly punished for tardiness, for not being tidy, and for being unprepared. It was difficult for me to find time in the busy, chore-filled evenings, to do my homework. The teachers looked at me with disgust rather than understanding; they were often furious at me for these things that were beyond my control.

I recall the English composition teacher who was always pulling my hair and slapping me just because she passed me in the hall. She was known for that. I wish I could meet her now as I would give her a slap back. There were forty-two of us girls in one room of the school. She would always find something wrong about me. If I could not finish my homework, she'd come running at me saying, "Look at this girl, look at this girl! She didn't do her homework." I'll never forget the day she took my book and threw it out the window on a rainy day. It got soaked through, so I got beaten at home.

But still I persisted. Even when I was very young, I somehow knew it would be worse to be poor and uneducated although it did seem they were doing everything to get me to drop out of school–both the teachers and my mother. It seemed so easy for them to smack me instead of offering me the slightest compassion. Some of the girls in my classes were kind. I remember friends would tear a page out of their books and give it to me so I could write and follow the lessons. Sometimes a friend would give me five cents for the bus or give me a lift with them in their cars. I lived in such a shadow of shame because of our poverty.

At home, I had to do everything. I had to take care of my baby sister, who arrived after Michael, and I would get beaten if she cried in the night. But I found some joy in the evenings. After cooking, I would put food on a big plate. My siblings and I shared this plate. I would take the plate to the sea, and I would sit facing the sea. My dream was to cross that sea and go to London, England one day. I had one spoon, and I placed them around me in a semi-circle. I would feed them a spoonful each and then lastly, I'd give myself a spoonful. I felt like an important big sister. We were together.

We lived in a primitive wooden house in a compound with other similar houses. There were often neighborhood gambling sessions with a whole bunch of men playing *mahjong* (dominoes in English). It still makes me cry to think of the time one of the men discovered they lost money and claimed I had stolen it. I had not. My mother and my aunt were so angry at me and did not believe me when I told them I had not even seen the money. They beat me with a bamboo cane. I kept telling them I had not taken anything, yet they kept beating me and asking me where the money was. My aunt had a great suggestion: "Tie her up!" she said.

I was tied up and they left me crying on the floor. They came back hours later saying: "Tell us you stole it. If you tell the truth, you won't get any more beatings."

In the end I said I did steal it even though I didn't. The beating stopped but now they were looking for the money. They searched my things, went through my schoolbooks and bags. They asked one of the kids my age to watch me at school, to check if I went into the tuck shop where they sold drinks and ice creams. The classmate reported back saying, no she didn't see me buy anything.

They kept asking me where I hid the money. I told them I didn't have the money as I didn't steal it. Eventually the people must have found the money, as my mother and aunt gave up. Today, almost sixty years later, I still get upset about this incident as I've never been a thief. It is a bitter memory as my heart still cannot understand why my mother did not protect me. It reminds me of that when you are poor, there is so much that people think about you and worse is what they do to you.

In the end, I had to leave school at age fifteen as there was no money for school fees and supplies. I cried as I really wanted to be somebody. My father took pity and gave me money to take a stenography course. I couldn't adapt to it; to me the markings all looked like bean sprouts. I dropped out of it and found work as a salesgirl in a department store.

I gave my earnings to my mother to help out with the kids, keeping only enough money to take the bus to work and back. One dollar was a lot of money as I could go to and from work and could get lunch with this small sum. When possible, I would do extra work for my neighbors, and I would keep that money. I had an ambition to be a beautician, so I was saving for school.

I had only two dresses to wear in the posh stores. I washed and dried them for the next day--ironing them stiffly so although old, the dresses looked good. I did well as a salesgirl as I knew the importance of looking neat and clean. I started to learn about makeup then. I loved how I looked with makeup and that is why I joined the cosmetic field.

I was hardworking, and the owner knew I was very interested, so she helped by enrolling me in a course. I finished the course and sold the company's cosmetics. I was always very busy. I asked for the samples they wanted to throw out and I'd take them home and use them. When I finished that class, I discovered there was a modeling class. Despite not being able to pay much, I was allowed to take the course. I learned how to walk and pose wearing fashionable clothing. We were shown how to pose to show designs on the dress, and how to highlight the accessories, such as shawls and jewelry.

After the course, I was delighted to be selected for a job with an advertising company. At that time, there were no big posters everywhere—most advertising was on the cinema screen. Before movies started, while waiting for the main feature, they showed those adverts. In my most famous advert for Dutch baby milk in powder form, I pretended to be a mother getting milk from the fridge to feed her baby. Somebody else did my makeup and I did my little act. I was so proud of it.

I met my husband who was a civil engineer from Norway shortly after I modelled. He traveled a lot and I went with him. Together we lived in Thailand, Singapore, Germany, Indonesia, Australia, and Sweden, often for two years at a time, then we moved to Norway to raise a family. Although I was so happy to start a new life with him in Norway, I was totally unprepared for the racism I would encounter there. It started with his mother. She was angry with him that he did not choose a European wife and she did not give me a chance. She did not even try to build a relationship with me. I hoped when we had our first child, his family would warm to us, but they did not. She could not accept me or my children because of my race.

It was worse outside of the family. Wealthy Norwegians were so disrespectful to me and were open in their disregard to my humanity and intelligence. They referred to me as a whore and would not let their children play with my son, openly referring to him as a "son of a whore" or "coffee bean" because of his color, making it a joke that he was coffee mixed with milk.

As my son had no one to play with, I played with him. We would go out to a field to play soccer and I would be the goalkeeper. But I wanted him to have all the advantages of his peers. After school, he was to stay later for piano lessons; I had to stop the lessons because another child would shoot an air gun at him as he walked home. My son was heartbroken and bewildered by his treatment. My daughter managed to make one friend, but that friend died in an accident not far from our home. After that horrendous incident, she did not mix with others.

In the end, I bought chocolates and distributed them to the local children. They played with him because of the chocolates, and this led to some true friendships. Later these boys started coming to our house as I made pizza. We had a big cellar, and the boys would go there and hang out. It wasn't long before most of his classmates would all gather at my house; I'd feed them breakfast or dinner. I didn't mind as my son now had friends, all the bullying stopped, and I knew where he was. They boys soon trusted me enough to tell me, apologetically, how they had bullied my children. Despite this, they were never allowed to invite my son to their houses. The children changed once they got to know us, but not their parents.

It was a hard life, but I had a lot of good things. As a wife to a manager, me and my children were not poor. We had a nice house, and all the consumer goods that the family of my birth could only dream of. As I was always a hard worker, I contributed by taking care of the family. But that alone was not enough for me; I also needed to bring money into the household. I had to work.

In 1977, I found work, first at a local gas station. I needed this extra money as I was determined that my children would have everything they wanted and they needed a lot to stay ahead of the bullies. All the other kids wore all kinds of branded clothing and other items. I was afraid for them; I knew what it was like to be judged as poor so I made sure they had as much or more than other kids so they would not be snubbed for not having the right stuff, as well as for being foreigners. I was afraid for them, particularly for my son. Clothing, jackets, shoes–I did that for him as I did not want him to be treated badly as he was the only foreigner there.

I found work with a company, now defunct, that sold books and magazines, chocolates, and food. We had contracts and we were supposed to get paid commissions. They cheated me; the company did not pay out my commissions. The district manager, a young punk who looked down on me, ignored my genuine efforts to do well in the job and did not offer me opportunities to advance or to get fair pay. The attitude was we immigrants didn't belong in Norway, so we were to accept being unfairly treated and manipulated—our commissions were less or were kept from us. I will never forgive them as I worked hard and did my best for them. Even the Norwegian white women were not treated as equal to the men.

I decided to start my own business. I made frequent trips to Malaysia and started to import ceramics and art to sell in Norway. I did this until I got sick with cancer and had to close it down as there was no one to take care of my businesses. But while I was working, I felt stronger and stronger inside. With my growing empowerment, in my heart were always the horrible names I had been called as a child and also by the Norwegian community as an adult. Thus, I noticed other immigrants, and could sense when some needed my help. I could not abide to see injustices such as that of immigrants being taken advantage of.

One of the things I am most proud of is I saved two men and three women from human trafficking, at great risk to myself. I was threatened frequently, and my husband feared I'd be murdered. One of the men I saved was from Pakistan, the second from Bangladesh. I discovered they were being manipulated and not paid. I spoke to other immigrants who looked miserable and found some Indonesian women who were brought in as domestic helpers but whose employers withheld their passports and their pay.

By this time, my children were grown: I was ready to be caught as to help these people at times I impersonated government officials and this is punishable with jail time. I ignored the threats to my freedom and my life as my kids did not depend on me anymore. I would pretend to be from a government department and tell the abusive employers I would report them unless they promised to send the victims back to their homes immediately, where they were desperate to return. The victims of this type of bullying were so grateful to me. They needed kind words, and they called me Aunty.

Doing charity work nourished my sad soul. I joined the international Rotary and was very involved in doing good work. I also created the International Women's Club, Pearl of the Orient, in Panang, Malaysia. Later I formed another one, the International Women's Club of Campoamor, in Spain.

I loved doing it, but I didn't see at first that I still was neglecting myself, not loving myself after a childhood of neglect and abuse. I didn't see this and then it was like I understood my sadness as clear as a bell. I heard it in my soul when someone said to me, "you are always doing things for other people and not for yourself." In order to feel deserving, I stayed busy, doing a lot of things for others.

In retirement and when I got ill, I had to slow down. I grew very depressed as I had too much time to think and no energy or requirement to do things. Every morning I woke up, I would sit in a chair and just cry. I grew anxious and would lay in bed and not feel able to leave the house. I couldn't understand why I could not move past my suffering. I felt something was bothering me, but I could not identify exactly what. The doctors gave me medication and went to a few therapists. After a few months, it would get better and then I'd go to another therapist.

In the last two years, before my husband got sick, I was managing to keep myself in good spirits, but the depression would come back. I found what provoked it was getting scolded, as that takes me right back to when I was young. In that kind of scenario, I don't know how to answer the person and I turn to mush. It is a horrible feeling as it brings back everything I have been through. I recently had this experience with a coach who is helping me start my business. It was bad, but I worked through it as I believe my new venture is very important.

I am now in my eighties and recently I've been spending a lot of time reflecting on my life. I can see how the work I've done for the Rotary helped to distract me from my pain but in full retirement, I kept thinking back to the way I have been treated as an Asian woman and then as an Asian woman living in the West. I realize that underneath my actions was this feeling that I was unworthy, so I was working so hard to earn respect from others and even from myself. It was like I needed to do things so I could be acknowledged as good, at least for all the good I have done in the world. I know now that one does not need to DO things to be a worthwhile person.

There is so much pain in the world, and the worst thing to be is poor and a girl. It is greater because we often feel like we have to ignore it, push it down, in order to get ahead in life. So that means later in life, when you may have less to do because you are retired or unwell in your old age, all you can do is think and this can lead to major depression. This happened to me.

I started an online group for older people so they can meet, and I can help them. I tell them that we all are worthwhile and deserve to have a great life. I remind them of that. I remind them to let go of old secrets and pain and to love themselves. I provide them with social activities online and companionship that serves me as much as it serves them. No matter your age, it is never too late to heal, it is never too late to learn to put yourself first. We all need to live our lives with more inner peace. I have found so much comfort in knowing others see me and value me just for being myself.

Help Her RECOVER

Sustainability is the key to our survival on this planet and will also determine success on all levels.

~ *Shari Arison*

Help Her Recover

By Amanda Willett

SUSTAINABILITY Principle 10, "I CAN CREATE A BALANCE BETWEEN STRUCTURE AND CHANGE," in the context of recovery, it emphasizes the importance of finding equilibrium between stability and transformation during the healing process. When recovering from trauma, particularly gender-based violence, survivors often need structure and stability as a foundation to rebuild their lives. This structure can include access to essential services like therapy, legal support, safe housing, and a supportive community. However, it's equally vital for survivors to embrace change, personal growth, and empowerment. Recovery isn't just about returning to the way things were before the trauma; it's about evolving into a healthier and stronger version of oneself. Thus, this principle encourages survivors to strike a balance between seeking the support and structure they need while also embracing opportunities for personal growth, healing, and advocating for systemic changes that prevent future violence. Ultimately, finding this equilibrium allows survivors to achieve long-term healing, resilience, and a renewed sense of agency over their lives.

Mary Anne's early life was marked by hardship, abuse, and discrimination. Growing up in a challenging environment where she had to take on adult responsibilities at a young age, she faced physical abuse, poverty, and racism. At the age of seven, she faced a life-threatening situation while washing diapers in a pond. A stranger intervened to save her, even though she initially perceived him as just another adult criticizing her. This incident highlights her ability to navigate difficult situations and make choices to ensure her survival, demonstrating her determination and resilience.

Mary Anne's childhood was marred by poverty, lack of access to education, and mistreatment by both family members and teachers. Despite these challenges, she persisted in her desire for education and self-improvement. She faced discrimination and bullying in Norway due to her race and ethnicity, even after moving there with her husband.

Survivors of gender-based violence must establish a foundation of safety, support, and healing, providing them with the necessary structure to rebuild their lives. Mary Anne's journey towards empowerment and sustainability began when she started working, eventually starting her own business. Through hard work and determination, she achieved financial independence and was able to provide for her family. However, she did not stop at personal success. She used her newfound empowerment to help others, especially immigrants who were victims of human trafficking and exploitation, often putting herself at risk to rescue them.

In her later years, Mary Anne continued her commitment to helping others by starting a group for older people to provide companionship and support. She recognized the importance of inner peace and self-worth, emphasizing that every individual deserves to be valued for who they are.

Mary Anne's life journey reflects the theme of sustainability in her ability to create a balance between structure (working for self-improvement and financial stability) and change (empowering others and advocating for their rights). She exemplifies the idea that personal growth and empowerment can lead to positive change not only for oneself but also for the community and society at large.

SUSTAINABILITY

Principle 10:
I CAN CREATE A BALANCE
BETWEEN STRUCTURE AND CHANGE

Write about your goals and aspirations.
How can you use structure to support your goals,
and how can you remain open to necessary
changes along the way?

Affirmation:

I welcome structure as a foundation for my goals, knowing it supports my journey of growth and transformation.

Tree Pose (Vrksansana)

Tree Pose is usually the first standing balance pose that is taught to yoga beginners because it's the simplest. Keep your sense of humor about learning to stand on one leg. It's harder than it looks at first and will be different every day. Don't get frustrated if you wobble or even fall over at first. Come to stand in Mountain Pose (Tadasana) with your hands in Anjali mudra at your heart center.

1. Take a moment to feel both your feet root into the floor, your weight distributed equally on all four corners of each foot.
2. Begin to shift your weight into your right foot, lifting your left foot off the floor. Keep your right leg straight but don't lock the knee.
3. Bend your left knee and bring the sole of your left foot high onto your inner right thigh.

4. Press your foot into your thigh and your thigh back into your foot with equal pressure. This will help you keep both hips squared toward the front so your right hip doesn't jut out.
5. Focus your gaze (Drishti) on something that doesn't move to help you keep your balance.
6. Take 5 to 10 breaths, then lower your left foot to the floor and do the other side.

Mindful Focusing Meditation:

Here's a mindful meditation practice to help you embody the theme of creating a balance between structure and change:

1. **Find a Quiet Space:** Begin by finding a quiet and comfortable place to sit or lie down. Ensure that you won't be disturbed during your meditation.
2. **Relax Your Body:** Close your eyes and take a few deep breaths. Inhale deeply through your nose, and exhale slowly through your mouth. As you exhale, let go of any tension in your body.
3. **Grounding Visualization:** Imagine yourself standing on a peaceful beach with the waves gently rolling in. Feel the stability of the sand beneath your feet. This beach symbolizes the balance between structure and change.
4. **Embrace Structure:** As you stand on the beach, bring your awareness to the concept of structure. Visualize it as a strong and steady lighthouse in the distance. This lighthouse represents the foundation and structure in your life.
5. **Breathe in Structure:** As you breathe in, imagine that you are inhaling the qualities of structure, organization, and stability. Feel these qualities filling you from head to toe, grounding you in the present moment.

6. **Embrace Change:** Now, shift your focus to the vast ocean in front of you. This represents the ever-changing and dynamic aspects of life. Acknowledge that change is a natural and neces- sary part of growth.
7. **Breathe in Change:** As you breathe in again, imagine that you are inhaling the qualities of change, adaptability, and transforma- tion. Feel these qualities flowing through you, invigorating your spirit.
8. **Balance Visualization:** Visualize a harmonious dance between the lighthouse of structure and the ever-flowing ocean of change. See how they complement each other, creating a sense of equilibrium in your life.
9. **Affirmation:** Repeat the affirmation silently or aloud: "I welcome structure as a foundation for my goals, knowing it supports my jour- ney of growth and transformation." Say this affirmation with sincer- ity, embracing both structure and change.
10. **Feel the Balance:** Sense the balance within you as you hold both structure and change in your awareness. Recognize that structure provides the stability you need to set and achieve your goals, while change offers the flexibility to adapt and evolve.
11. **Gratitude:** Express gratitude for this moment of balance and under- standing. Acknowledge the importance of structure in your life's journey.
12. **Silent Reflection:** Sit in silence for a few minutes, allowing the feel- ing of balance to resonate within you. Reflect on how you can apply this balance to your goals and aspirations.
13. **Closing:** When you're ready to conclude your meditation, slowly open your eyes. Carry the sense of balance between struc- ture and change with you as you navigate your path forward.

RITUALS FOR Recovery

This meditation practice helps you cultivate a sense of balance between structure and change in your life. By visualizing and affirming the importance of both elements, you create a foundation that supports your goals and personal growth, while also embracing the adaptability needed for transformation. This balance can guide your decision-making and help you navigate life's transitions with grace and resilience.

SPEAK OUT

SARAH LEWIS

Sarah (she/her) is an Anishnaabe Kwe (Ojibwe/Cree) spoken word artist, activist, musician, community organizer and mother from Curve Lake First Nation, Ontario, Canada. She was appointed as Peterborough's inaugural Poet Laureate in 2021 and has been featured on CBC Arts, Global News, and stages across the world.

Sarah utilizes poetry as an act of resistance. Giving voice to the resurgence of Indigenous communities and how Indigenous people are reclaiming their identities, culture, strength, and sovereignty. She encourages other aspiring poets to speak their truth, and to envision and work towards a decolonial society where sexism, the patriarchy, capitalism and racism do not exist.

KEEP USING YOUR VOICE
By
Sarah Lewis

The strength of our Indigenous communities is woven into the very fabric of our existence, and the loss of our women is a wound that strikes deep into the heart of who we are as a people.

—Eden Robinson

Aniin/Hello

Right now, as I write this, I sit at the shore of Henry's Gaaming, a beach in my home community of Curve Lake First Nation. I'm burning sage, as specs of sand and cold air brush my skin. I reminisce about all of the memories, little and big moments, dreams, and callings that have led me back to this land, to this water, to this space in time, to this pen and paper, preparing to tell you my journey of pain, resilience, hope and most importantly–healing. I have tears in my eyes because it has and continues to be both a scary and beautiful journey.

This water reminds me of my journey. Tonight, there are calm waters that meet the sunset, radiating the bittersweet end to summer. Periodically, there are bumpy waters when a fishing boat speeds by and some days the waves come crashing in on the shore, reminding us of the power and strength that she holds. Nonetheless, she is forever changing, resting, flowing, moving, and healing our people.

Anishnaabemowin women have been praying for Nibi (water) for millennia. We've always known that this water is our kin, is sacred, alive and has the capacity to heal and take care of our people. All living things in our natural world are interconnected and can be great teachers of wisdom if we take a moment to sit and listen to what they have to say and do. Colonization of the land, Indigenous bodies and water is the reason why a lot of our teachings have been buried or forgotten. This is why we've also stopped listening to the water, the trees and all our relations in nature. But this land and water helps us to remember. Reminds us that this is our home, reminds us that telling our stories is an act of resistance as we continue to unearth these teachings, and use our voices to create political change in our communities and nations.

As my kin, I'd like to think that I too hold this same magic and capability as Nibi. I'd like to think that I carry not only the intergenerational trauma of my ancestors, land, and water– but the resiliency, healing, and strength of them as well. We are not separate, and like Nibi, our actions and life experiences have ripple effects to those around us and to the future generations. So it is important we keep trying to unlearn harmful colonial belief systems to not only heal our traumas but so our future kin and collective communities can also thrive. This truth became even more vital as soon as I became a mother at the age of twenty-two. Not only would my actions affect my own journey but now another little life relied on me for support and guidance as they navigate through this bumpy yet beautiful thing we call life.

So where do we begin? How do we pave the way for these future generations? I believe that we create safe spaces possible for change when we listen to someone's voice. The importance of listening to someone's story of hardship, beauty, hopes, and dreams is how we can better connect and relate to one another while nurturing community.

In my chapter, I will be discussing what spoken word poetry is, how it has forever transformed my life and ultimately the power of voice.

Since everything is interconnected, to understand my story better, it is important to acknowledge and understand those who came before me. A part of my story includes shining light on the past. It is important to note that Indigenous people in Canada have been silenced for decades, and I believe this is why I have always loved the art of spoken word poetry. When an opportunity arises to use my voice and to tell my story, I jump at it because I know that not everyone has the opportunity to do so. This story is not mine alone, but what many Indigenous people have experienced, continue to experience, but most importantly how we can all continue to heal and grow together.

This is for the ancestors who continuously guide me back to my purpose and my power.

My path to healing began on the rez roads of Curve Lake First Nation, Ontario and Pukatawagon, Manitoba. These streets are important because they are what would spark the desire for change I wanted to see amongst my communities. These are the streetlights that would guide me to my voice, my calling and light the path for others to do so as well.

The "rez" or reservation is the result of colonization. The desire to own the land and extract its resources and means to achieve that resulted in a mass genocide of Indigenous peoples on Turtle Island or so called "Canada." To combat the resistance from Indigenous people to give up the land they hunted, gathered, and relied on for millennia they created small 'reservations' for Indigenous people to live on—often far away from developing colonies and often unfarmable and uninhabitable.

Pre colonization, Indigenous people shared this land, stretching from coast to coast. We didn't view the land as something you possess or own, it is a gift to be honored and protected. Mother earth is an entity that we rely on for life, she is the mother of all humans. So when you colonize the land, you colonize our bodies. If you take away the birthing place of our livelihoods, where we hunt, fish, breathe, you take a part of ourselves away. We are not separate. I think this applies to the ongoing colonization of Indigenous women's bodies as well.

Systemic racism and view of Indigenous women as subhuman has resulted in an overrepresentation of missing and murdered women in Canada where Indigenous women are four times more likely to go missing or be murdered than non-indigenous women. limitations caused by the fact that the data collected is based on incidents reported to police. However, Native Women's Association of Canada states that "community-based research has found levels of violence against Aboriginal women to be even higher than those reported by government surveys. Government officials, RCMP and police are just as much a part of the problem as they have failed to protect our women and girls. Many Indigenous families consistently report RCMP's and Police's inability to prioritize their cases due to racial stereotyping and stigma to their lifestyles stating: "Oh, she's just a prostitute, she's probably just on a binge, she'll come home," was the police response, according to Bruyere from a CBC news report in 2015. Even more ignored and overlooked, are women involved in the sex trade, where between 1991 and 2004, one hundred seventy-one women were murdered in Canada and forty-five percent of the cases remain unresolved according to Statistics Canada in 2016.

Residential schools were also the result of colonization which would cause huge ramifications affecting our people for decades to come. In addition, the government of Canada created Indian residential schools that would be run by the catholic churches. From 1831 to 1996, Indigenous children were mandated to live at these facilities year-round. The goal was to assimilate the children to Canadian culture and "take the Indian out of the child." Indigenous people were banned from practicing their culture, ceremonies or speaking their language. Those who did so were killed, punished, or incarcerated. They knew our strength, identity and power was in our teachings and our culture and the best way to achieve power was to strip us of ours.

It is estimated that over six thousand children never made it home, and those who did would carry that trauma from all of the sexual, physical, verbal and cultural abuse that took place at these "schools."

My people often turned to self-medicating with alcohol to numb and forget what happened, these coping mechanisms were also passed down our family lines.

Although uncomfortable, providing historical context is an instrumental process as we move towards truth and reconciliation. Reconciliation between settlers and Indigenous women is not possible without truth first. "Nobody's free until everybody's free" – Fannie Lou Hamer. And as matriarch Lilla Watson once said: "If you have come here to help me you are wasting your time, but if you have come because your liberation is bound up with mine, then let us work together."

These subjects are the driving forces as to why I ultimately chose to become a spoken word poet, but most importantly to remind all women that we are more than our trauma and what has happened to us and healing is possible even after our worlds have felt like they have been shattered and shaken. My people are proof of this. I am proof of this. You are proof of this.

Looking back, I didn't understand the complexities and rationale as to why my family and community members struggled with addiction and violence so intensely. I had internalized the racism I had experienced growing up and figured I was doomed to be just another drunk Indian incapable of fitting in with society. I was penalized by my own peers about the darkness of my skin and would hide from the sun. I didn't know who I was, I never felt comfortable in my skin. I eventually turned to alcohol at age thirteen and became the self-fulfilling prophecy I dreamt into existence. It made me feel numb and I finally felt confident in my skin– or so I thought. Over the years, my drinking became more and more frequent, and I would continue to struggle with alcoholism into adulthood.

I had always felt like an artist at heart, and was generally good at playing musical instruments, drawing, painting, singing and so on.

However, it wasn't until grade 11 that I would discover my niche. I attended a two-day intro to spoken word workshop with prolific spoken word poet and slam poet Zacheaus Jackson. The way he eloquently yet powerfully told his story with such cadence, intensity, rhythm, speed, vulnerability, and truth inspired me. I only knew poetry from the Shakespearean books we skimmed in middle school, and I didn't have much care for it as I couldn't relate or understand it. However, this version of poetry blew me away. Spoken word poetry is exactly how it sounds; it is poetry that is spoken out loud. There are a number of techniques, tricks, and tools to improve the delivery and way you present it, but essentially you can tell your story however you want and speak about whatever you please. Again, typically the themes amongst spoken word artists tend to be more political, and I think there is a reason for that. Slam poetry was created in the 80s in Chicago by the BIPOC (Black, Indigenous, people of color) community. These spaces and stages gave people a voice, voices that have again, been historically silenced.

That being said, I think what made the biggest impression on me was that for the first time, I had heard my own story being told. Where there was shame about what it means to be Indigenous, now stood connection and an acknowledgement of my truth through someone else's experience. I didn't feel alone in my trauma or the violence I had experienced. He made me feel like there was hope beyond the trauma. He preached that this art form saved his life, and to this day I really do think art holds the capacity to save lives. Zacheus was a young Indigenous man who lived on the downtown east side of Vancouver. Like me, he struggled with repercussions of colonialism, displacement from his homelands, loss of culture and identity. He was a crack addict who stumbled into a venue one evening and discovered his niche that night as well.

Maybe this was our destiny, our mission, written in the stars and we were the messengers from the ancestors. Afterall, our ancestors were storytellers. Our teachings and knowledge were passed down through oral tradition. We've been storytelling since we were wished into existence by our creator.

If someone would have told this quiet little girl who hated public speaking that I would end up sharing my truth with thousands of people across the globe, that I would be featured on television, news, newspapers, radios, books, websites, that I would become Peterborough's Inaugural Poet Laureate, hosting workshops, speaking in front of city council, for schools, writing my first book and traveling across the world because of my poetry and so much more...

I would laugh! This truly was divine guidance from my ancestors. I feel they co created, dreamt, and prayed this story into existence. I have always felt like they have guided and nudged me towards this path, as though there is a grander scheme other than just writing poetry. Opportunities have risen because I feel a part of my purpose is much bigger than myself– but to remind people of our truth, and even more, to spark conversations about how we can heal and move forward together in community.

I feel I am also here to talk about all of the missing and murdered Indigenous women. To give voice to Theresa Merasty, my late auntie who went missing, was murdered, and found on the infamous Highway of Tears in British Columbia– a stretch of highway known for hitchhiker women disappearing on. I talk about my Indigenous sisters/classmates/friends that went missing and were murdered. I say their names– Leah Anderson, Kara Fosseneuve, Ashley Bear, and Cileanna Taylor. These were girls and women who had dreams, who were sisters, daughters, were life givers and most importantly humans that have names and faces. They are not just another statistic. That should be enough. We don't have to prove our humanness to you, citizens in Canada, government officials, and police need to prove to us that they care and do the work, so our sisters stop dying. People ask how they can help, and I always ask them to refer to the 231 Calls to Justice: Reclaiming Power and Place. Everything has been outlined in this *Final Report of the National Inquiry into Missing and Murdered Indigenous Women and Girls*, which delivers two hundred thirty-one individual calls for justice directed at governments, institutions, social service providers, industries, and all Canadians. According to the National Family and Services Circle, "these calls for Justice are legal imperatives and represent important ways to end the genocide and to transform systemic and societal values that have worked to maintain colonial violence". You can locate the digital report at: www.familysurvivalcircle.ca

All this to say, I think spirit works in magical ways and so when you reach out to the higher realms and ask how you can help, how you can heal not only yourself but your communities in which you are a part of– be prepared for an answer and a plan.

I now teach workshops for people at all different ages. I remind participants that we all have a story, each story is unique, and it is worth telling. Writing, preparing, and presenting can be a somatic healing experience. A story risen from the ashes, the dust, and dirt can feel like a cathartic release. A letting go of something that was stuck in your head and body, now onto paper and even onto a stage potentially. And as mentioned previously, this sharing of humanness and experience can also foster connection and community.

There are many different artistic ways to express yourself, spoken word poetry just happened to be the medium that I was most drawn to. This was a medium where I could talk about the violence I and so many other Indigenous women and girls had experienced, discuss solutions and ways to heal. The impact that spoken word poetry has can manifest in a number of ways. A lot of the time, my goal is to implant a thought or perspective that my listeners may have never heard before. Planting that seed, has the power to spark more conversations about the issue, raise awareness to eventually take action and plan for resolution.

For me, I find that there is not any designated time and place where the inspiration to write strikes. It comes to me whenever I feel inspired, and typically this is after listening to other poets or public speakers share on world issues, listening to inspiring music, going for walks, sitting in nature, etc. Nature really is a meditative space for me where inspiration has always flowed naturally. As mentioned before, we are all connected. This is your kin– the trees, grass, wind, crickets are your cousins. The land is your home, and the creatures and plants are your relatives. So, feeling safe and grounded will nurture that creativity as well. Once I feel enough motivation, I let all of the ideas flow from my mind onto a piece of paper or in the notes section in my phone and begin the brainstorming process. It takes many edits, thoughtfulness, reviewing, and reciting until I finally come up with something I like.

I suggest writing about something that moves you. What if you were leaving tomorrow, and you only had one more story to tell, that you absolutely needed the world to hear– what would it be? Think about the thing that makes you get up in the morning, or the thing that changed your life forever, be it good or bad. These are the pieces that people remember. I think a large part of what makes a spoken word impactful as well is the emotion behind it. Hearing someone share their story with all that emotion and authenticity is so powerful to watch. I can't count the amount of times I have gotten goose bumps or cried after hearing a poet share a piece of themselves on those stages.

I would suggest searching for other poets and storytellers in your community. If there are no groups, events, or places where poets gather, take the initiative and start your own group! Again, it does not necessarily have to be poetry. If your passion is painting, photography, fashion, singing, playing an instrument, dance, or theatre– roll with that and seek out places where you can safely express yourself and share your stories.

It is important to remember that we are all creators. We are all artists at heart. Never forget that. You need to throw away the idea of imperfection and create solely to create. You're allowed to just exist, to just *be*. You don't need to be an award-winning artist to release or share your work. I think we have gotten trapped in the idea that our work needs to be monetized to be deemed worthy of sharing with the world. I challenge you to unlearn this colonial thought process. Paint whatever you want in whatever way. Write about whatever your beautiful heart desires. There is no rule book or prescription for this stuff. The only rule is that you have to try. You have to try because art is what moves the world, what makes life beautiful, what has inspired and made cultures thrive for thousands of years.

Another important element I want to talk about is the former coping mechanism piece. As mentioned earlier, I dealt with my trauma by numbing my emotions and uncomfortability with life. If you've ever dealt with substance abuse, you will understand that it carries a lot of stigma. I've shamed myself so many times and have talked to myself in ways that I would never talk to another human. Over time I have had to forgive myself. Forgive myself for doing what I had to do to survive. This is what I knew, with the resources that I had that time, and I did my best. Although tough, addiction has also been a teacher for me. It has taught me that intergenerational habits are a thing, that our children are watching what we do. I only knew of alcohol because everyone in my family drank around me. It was and continues to be romanticized in the media, society, and even in my own community. That said, I have the power to end this generational cycle, so that my son and those who come after me can thrive. I have the power to break the cycle of addiction in my family. I also learned that I am avoidant and do not like to deal with conflict or any uncomfortable emotion. Facing these fears is what has ultimately helped me feel them and overcome them.

Over time I have been able to develop a number of "rituals" I use daily and when I am experiencing uncomfortable emotions. I will share with you one of the rituals I practice when my spirit needs nourishment. It is a meditation/prayer ritual I usually try to do at the beginning of my day, as it sets the tone for your day.

1. Begin by finding a quiet comfortable spot to sit. If possible, find a place outside close to nature– in the grass, or near a tree or body of water.

2. Light a candle, and light sage to smudge your space. Smudging is a therapeutic ritual in my culture whereby you light the white sage, waving a feather or your hand over the smoke and over your body/mind/spirit and space to cleanse it. The medicine cleans your body, spirit, and space of negativity. In addition to this, sometimes I will light sweetgrass. This is another one of our four medicines, and in contrast, welcomes positivity into the space when lit and smudged.

3. Begin by welcoming your spirit guides, ancestors, and anyone significant to you that has passed on into the space.

4. Thank them for guiding and watching over you, reveal anything you want to share or anything difficult that you might be going through, ask for further guidance, protection, any answers you might seek. Pray for any other loved one's protection. Ask for motivation, inspiration, and energy throughout your day. Ask for support in moving through any potential uncomfortable emotions and situations throughout the day. Set any intentions or goals you may want to accomplish and ask to be supported in these intentions and goals. Ask for bravery or courage if you need it, and anything else you might need. Our helpers are always listening! They are always supporting us even when we can't see them. If I'm wanting more precise answers, sometimes I will additionally draw one to three cards from my oracle deck. Your spirit guides will reach you through these cards as well. You can purchase these at most book or spiritual stores.

5. Lighting the sage once more, you then say thank you, I love you and am so grateful for your love and guidance always.

6. After this, begin listing all the things in your life that you are grateful for. The hope is that you begin to raise your vibrational frequency. When we list the things we are grateful for, by the laws of the universe, we attract more abundance and more

things to be grateful for. When we feel grounded, connected to those in the other realms, and gratitude will create a surge of love and joy through your body.

7. Blow out the candle and move into your day with all of this good medicine.

And because this is a book on healing and recovering from GBV, it is important to note that healing is not linear. You don't learn all the tips and tools in one day or week and you're all set for the rest of your life trauma free. I have staggered away from my path many times and needed reminders and maybe new ways of healing as I enter new stages and places in my life. I have experienced new traumas, some more easy to recover from, and some that take more attention and care. I have had traumas that come up years later, just when I think I have conquered an anxiety, trigger or fear, something new comes up and I have to revisit the event with compassion. We will continue to heal and grow on our journeys until the day we die. It is not about striving for a life of no pain, sadness, or fear, but how we cope and move through those traumatic events and understand that it gets easier with time and practice. I still have work ahead of me and that's okay. As long as I have hope, there is healing, as long as I keep picking myself back up, there is work to do. I am doing my best. I speak kind words to myself and give myself a break because I am doing my best. I practice mantras daily, because sometimes my mean thoughts are louder than the kind ones. This all takes practice, but like exercising a muscle it will become stronger and easier over time.

As I continue to do the work to heal, I often think about the prophecy of 'The Seventh Fire'. Elders in my community have taught me that with every choice or action you take, you need to think about how it will affect the seven generations that come after you. With our actions and daily rituals to healing, I believe we have the power to heal not only ourselves but those who come after us.

This book proves that we are stronger together. With each story interwoven with what has happened to us, we all know that this is not the important part. It is how we have transformed this pain and even intergenerational pain into poetry, into passion and into a success story. The stories we tell, and the action of reclaiming your power can transform the lives of those around you.

That said, I recognize that my actions and hard work is what has gotten me to where I am today, yet I still have to lend some of this credit to my spirit guides. It was only last year I had this certain aha moment, as I stepped into the honorary role as Peterborough's first Poet Laureate. I was to be the ambassador of the arts community and more specifically the poetry community. I never in my wildest dreams would have predicted I would achieve this. Moments after, I recalled a memory from five years prior. At this time, I was a newly sober single soon to be mother, feeling alone, not really sure where to go next. However, that day I was drawn to attend a psychic fair that was taking place in the city. Upon leaving, a woman waved me down and begged me to come to her booth. Thinking it was another person wanting me to purchase their services I told them I was just leaving, and I had somewhere to be. She demanded I stay a moment and was not asking for my money, but she said she had something important to tell me. She proclaimed: "you have hundreds of ancestors behind you cheering you on, guiding you… hundreds. Your throat chakra is lighting up, and they are telling me that whatever you do with your life, a part of your purpose is to use your voice, you need to continue to use your voice."

Years later, I would cry because I had only then realized what she had meant. I had never done poetry previous to this woman's premonition and didn't realize how I was going to "use my voice" or I didn't understand what that fully meant yet. The ancestors begged this woman to deliver this message and I am forever thankful. I asked and I received. You are always being guided from those on the other side.

Guided to tell your story, to heal, and to follow your purpose. When we pay attention to the little things and don't label them as coincidence, we find magic and guidance.

Right now, as I write this, I sit at the shore of Henry's Gaaming, a beach in my home community of Curve Lake First Nation. I put out my sage, and the smoke billows into the stars. I put my pen down as my story comes to a close.

>till Nibi and I meet again
>whether it be in shower, river, cup, eyes
>till she reminds me of all my relations, be it the sycamore trees, reeds, sky, like the leaves
>there have been many versions of me who have died and were rebirthed again
>there have been many versions of me who have died and were rebirthed again
>
>like the forest that has been cut down and burnt
>she rises again
>she rises again
>you will rise again
>you will rise again
>
>till the swift currents and tides pull me under
>reminding me to appreciate breath
>I don't hold it anymore because it was never mine to keep
>promises to keep coming back so as long as i keep my word
>keep releasing breath
>keep using voice
>keep using your voice
>Miigwetch

Help Her RECOVER

In every crisis, doubt, or confusion, take the higher path - the path of compassion, courage, understanding, and love.

~ *Amit Ray*

Help Her Recover

By Amanda Willett

COMPASSION Principle 11, "I HONOR THE INDIVIDUAL PATH OF RECOVERY AND GROWTH," underscores the importance of recognizing that each survivor's journey toward healing from gender-based violence is unique and deeply personal. It encourages compassion and empathy in supporting survivors as they navigate their own paths to recovery. This principle acknowledges that there is no one-size-fits-all approach to healing and that survivors should be respected for their resilience and courage in finding their way forward. By honoring the individuality of each survivor's experience and choices, we create a space where they can heal at their own pace, make their own decisions, and regain a sense of control over their lives. This principle reminds us that true support means standing alongside survivors with unwavering respect for their autonomy and strength.

Sarah Lewis takes us on a journey through her life, reflecting on her experiences as an Indigenous woman and how she found healing, purpose, and resilience through spoken word poetry. Here's a summary of the chapter and its connection to the theme:

In this chapter, Sarah Lewis begins by setting the scene at Henry's Gaaming, a beach in her home community of Curve Lake First Nation. She uses this natural backdrop to draw parallels between her life journey and the ever-changing nature of water. She reflects on the deep spiritual connection that Indigenous people have with nature, particularly with water (Nibi), as a source of healing and wisdom.

Sarah emphasizes how colonization has silenced Indigenous voices and disconnected them from their ancestral teachings. She underlines the importance of reestablishing this connection and reclaiming their stories as an act of resistance and healing. Becoming a mother at a young age added a new dimension to her journey, as she realized the impact of her actions on future generations.

The core message of this chapter revolves around the power of using one's voice. Sarah discusses her discovery of spoken word poetry and how it allowed her to tell her own story, to be heard, and nect with others who had similar experiences.

She points out that Indigenous people in Canada have been silenced for decades, and spoken word poetry provided a platform to break this silence and shed light on the shared traumas and struggles.

Sarah acknowledges the historical context of colonization, including the establishment of reservations and the devastating impact of residential schools. She highlights the importance of acknowledging this painful history as a vital step toward truth and reconciliation. By sharing her story through spoken word poetry, she aims to remind Indigenous women that they are more than their trauma and that healing is possible.

Sarah's personal journey from struggling with addiction to discovering her passion for spoken word poetry is a testament to the transformative power of art and storytelling. She believes that art can save lives and that it has the potential to raise awareness, spark conversations, and inspire positive change.

The chapter also emphasizes the importance of community and connection. Sarah encourages individuals to find their unique ways of expression, whether through poetry, painting, music, or other forms of art. She reminds readers that they are all creators and that their stories are worth sharing, regardless of whether they are award-winning artists.

Sarah Lewis concludes by emphasizing that healing is not a linear process. It requires ongoing effort, self-compassion, and a willingness to face uncomfortable emotions. She shares a meditation/prayer ritual that she practices daily to nourish her spirit, connecting with her ancestors and setting intentions for healing and growth.

In closing, Sarah Lewis's chapter beautifully illustrates the principle of honoring the individual path of recovery and growth.

Her journey of using her voice through spoken word poetry, reconnecting with her Indigenous roots, and advocating for missing and murdered Indigenous women serves as a powerful example of resilience, compassion, and the transformative potential of storytelling and art in the process of healing and recovery.

COMPASSION

Principle 11:
I HONOR THE INDIVIDUAL PATH OF
RECOVERY AND GROWTH

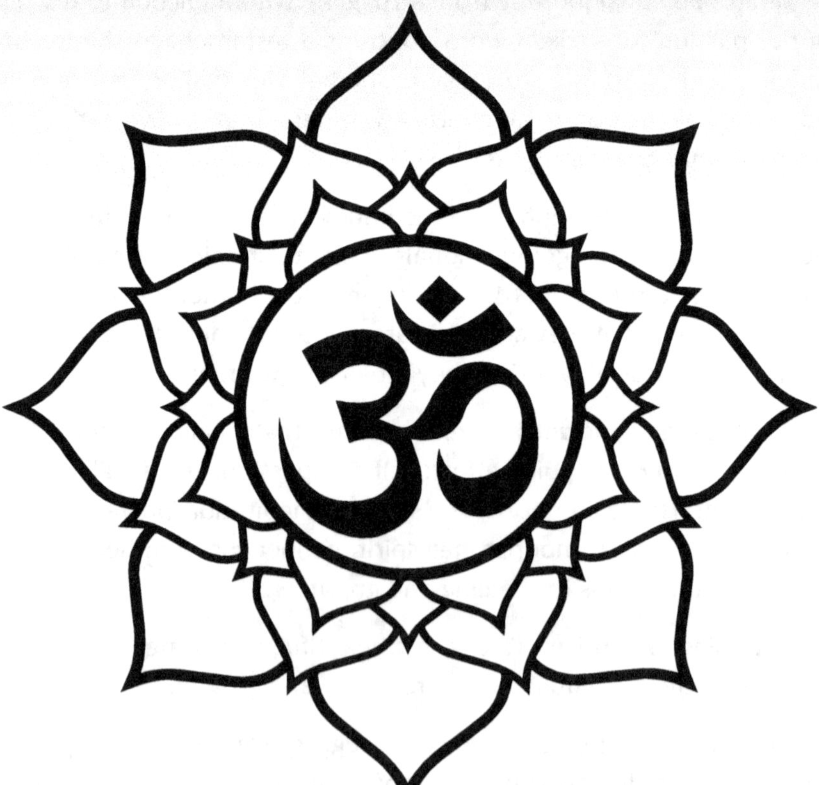

Reflect on the importance of self-compassion.
How can you be more compassionate toward yourself
as you navigate your unique journey?

Rituals for Recovery

Affirmation:

I extend kindness and empathy to myself, acknowledging that my path is a work in progress.

Warrior 1 (Virabhadrasana 1)

Set Up

Start in mountain pose. Step your left foot back three to four feet and place it down at a 45-degree angle. Ideally, your back left arch should be in line with your right heel, but you can separate your feet more to give yourself a wider base of support.

Keep your chest and hips facing forward to the front of the mat. Bend your front knee to a 90-de- gree angle directly over the ankle, with your toes pointing forward. Don't bend the knee past the ankle.

Getting Into the Pose

Press your back foot into the ground. Lengthen your spine and engage your core.

On an inhale, sweep the arms forward and up alongside the ears, palms facing each other.

Alignment

Stabilize the legs by pressing the left thigh back and pressing the left heel firmly into the mat.

Square the chest and hip to the front of the mat.

Keep your arms in line with your ears, engage your triceps, and press your shoulders down and away from the ears. Look forward or up toward the hands.

Mindful Focusing Meditation:

Here's a mindful meditation practice for the theme of compas- sion and honoring your individual path of recovery and growth:

Duration: 10-15 minutes (adjust as needed)

Instructions:

1. **Find a Quiet Space:** Choose a quiet and comfortable place where you won't be disturbed. Sit in a chair or on the floor with your back straight but not rigid, and your hands resting on your lap or knees.
2. **Relaxation:** Take a few deep breaths to settle into the present moment. As you exhale, release any tension in your body. Allow your breath to return to its natural rhythm.
3. **Focus on Breath:** Bring your attention to your breath. Observe the natural flow of your breath as it moves in and out of your body. Notice the rise and fall of your chest or the sensation of your breath at the nostrils.

RITUALS FOR Recovery

4. **Acknowledge Your Path:** Begin by acknowledging that you are on a journey of recovery and personal growth. Recognize that it's okay to be where you are right now, and that your path is unique to you.

5. **Self-Compassion Mantra:** Inhale deeply, and as you exhale, silently repeat a self-compassion mantra such as:
   - "I am deserving of love and kindness."
   - "I honor my journey of recovery."
   - "I extend empathy to myself as I grow."

6. **Visualize Warmth:** Imagine a warm, soft light surrounding you. This light represents the love and compassion you have for yourself. Visualize it expanding with each breath, filling your entire being with warmth and acceptance.

7. **Repeat Mantras:** Continue to repeat self-compassion mantras as you breathe. With each repetition, try to cultivate a sense of self-compassion, understanding, and acceptance.

8. **Embrace Imperfections:** Remind yourself that imperfections and setbacks are a natural part of growth. Rather than judging yourself harshly, embrace these moments with kindness and forgiveness.

9. **Sending Compassion:** Extend this compassion beyond yourself. Imagine sending love and kindness to others who may be on their own journeys of recovery and growth. Visualize them surrounded by the same warm light of compassion.

10. **Deepen the Breath:** Take a few deep breaths to conclude the practice. As you inhale, feel a sense of renewal and self-com- passion. As you exhale, release any remaining tension or self-crit- icism.

11. **Express Gratitude:** Before concluding, take a moment to express gratitude to yourself for dedicating time to this practice of self-compassion.

12. **Return to the Present:** Gently open your eyes if they were closed. Sit quietly for a few moments, feeling the effects of the practice, and carry this sense of self-compassion with you as you go about your day.

This meditation practice can help you develop a deeper sense of self-compassion and acceptance as you honor your unique journey of recovery and growth. You can return to this practice whenever you feel the need to reconnect with self-compassion and kindness.

SPEAK OUT

JENNY ROSS

Jenny is an engineer, parent, and politician. Eleven years ago, she was in a nineteen-year marriage to an abusive, mentally-ill man. Since then she has advocated for changes in how domestic violence cases are handled by advocacy organizations, clergy, and the courts. Jenny, a mom of two, lives in Illinois, USA with her two rescued hunting dogs, Lennie and Gail.

SHATTERED ILLUSIONS: FROM FAIRY TALE FAMILY TO MENTAL HEALTH DOMESTIC NIGHTMARE

By

Jenny Ross

I was living a life of death. I didn't exist. But I survived it. And when I walked out, I walked. And I didn't look back.

—Tina Turner

It was a magical November evening in Mount Prospect, Illinois; close enough to Christmas for the holiday lights to be on but still not bitterly cold. The lights added a bright and festive touch to the train station and dark brick buildings that surrounded it as I searched for a parking space. I finally found one and walked the few blocks to the restaurant in a swirling cloud of snowflakes. Once there, I joined a group of women from the local chapter of the Society of Women Engineers (SWE) for a holiday dinner.

At dinner, people talked about their holiday plans, their jobs, and their families. Some of the women were looking for new jobs, others had just started their first job after college. A few were older women, like me, with children in college and well-established careers. We talked and ate Mexican food carefully prepared to appeal to Midwestern palates in a back room that reminded me of the place where my former brother-in-law had his wedding rehearsal dinner.

I left as soon as I finished eating. I had come straight from work and needed to go home and feed my dogs. A few of the others left at the same time, hurrying to get home to pets or children while the others ordered another round of drinks or dessert and stayed to talk. The snow had stopped; the evening was colder and darker as I walked back to my car. I passed other people on the street, heading to dinner or drinks at one of the many restaurants in the area. I was glad that I came. I had enjoyed the evening. I found my car at the train station and got in.

Cloud cover blocked the star and moonlight, so it was very dark as I headed towards the tollway. There wasn't much traffic and it was a route that I had driven hundreds of times before, but it felt different. I started to feel uneasy and then I was overwhelmed by terror. I physically froze. Something about the evening had triggered a subconscious response. While my brain insisted that I had to pay attention to the road and to focus on driving, my body refused. I knew I couldn't let the fear engulf me completely and started to focus on my fingers and how each one felt on the steering wheel of the car, how my foot felt on the accelerator, how the seat felt against my body, what words were being said on the radio. Pulling myself back to the present moment helped; I felt the fear recede.

Later at home, I thought about the feeling of absolute terror that had taken over me in the car. I flashed back twenty years before, where on a similar night, I had gone downtown and met my then-husband, Mike, at a party associated with his work. I had left my job early, picked up the kids from daycare, met the babysitter, driven to the train station, taken the train downtown, and then taken a cab to meet him. He was irritated when I arrived because it had taken longer than he thought it should have for me to get there. There was alcohol at the event and we each had a couple of drinks. We were slightly drunk when we got on the train to go home.

Mike had lived in the Chicago suburbs for most of his life. At the time, although I had been there a few years, I still got lost. It was hard to hear the train conductor's announcements and I was nervous about missing our stop. After one almost unintelligible announcement, I asked Mike if we were close. He said yes, and we got off the train at the next stop only to find out that we were in the wrong place. We had gotten off in Golf, a small, wealthy suburb with a glass enclosed space for passengers to wait out of the weather, but no real train station. It was late at night, it was cold, and the next train wasn't going to come for at least an hour. We were the only ones there. We headed into the glass enclosure to get out of the wind.

Mike was furious and began yelling at me, telling me it was my fault. I opened my purse and got out my old Motorola flip phone, so I could call information and find a cab to take us to our car. Mike put his hands on my shoulders and shoved me into the glass wall of the train station, and I fell to the ground. I could not believe it—he had shoved me and thrown things at me many times at home, but this was the first time he had done it in a public place. Plus he shoved me while I was making an effort to find us a way to get back to the car and get home to our children. . When I looked up at his face it was full of hatred and anger. He didn't reach out to help me up, didn't say he was sorry, and didn't acknowledge that he had any part of getting off the train at the wrong stop.

I stood up, stepped away from him, and took a deep breath. I flipped open the phone, first calling information for a cab company phone number, then calling the cab company, and finally calling the babysitter. Mike watched me, his face twisted with hate and anger. He didn't say anything and didn't reach out to touch me again. We waited in silence for the cab, his body tense the entire time. Without talking, we got into the cab, got our car, and drove home. My body ached, my neck was sore, my shoulders hurt; I was sure that there were bruises forming under my clothes.

When we got home, Mike took the babysitter home and I checked on the kids, the dogs, and the cats. I had gone to bed by the time he came home. We never spoke of that evening again and I never went back to Golf. Unconsciously, I avoided ever being at a suburban train station at night, one of the many coping mechanisms I adopted to avoid confronting the trauma I experienced as a result of his emotional and physical abuse throughout our nineteen-year marriage.

From Fairy-Tale Perfect to Nightmare in the Suburbs

When Mike and I met in 1991, everything seemed perfect. We were introduced by mutual friends when I was on a work trip to Virginia where he lived. We started a long-distance relationship right away—me in Arizona, and Mike in Virginia. My parents and his parents had married after short courtships, so no one saw anything wrong with us deciding to marry soon after we met. I worked for the US Air Force, and he was an Air Force officer. I had an opportunity to move to a new job near him and within a year, I had moved to Virginia, gotten married, and was pregnant with our son.

A few years later, he decided to take a separation bonus and leave the military. We moved to northern Illinois to be closer to his extended family. There we bought a house and had another child. It all seemed fairy-tale perfect, but soon after our daughter was born in 1995, Mike had a psychotic break and started to hear voices coming from the upstairs hallway. The voices told him that I was having an affair and he was not the father of our daughter. He obsessively searched for proof of his delusions.

He was diagnosed with a psychotic illness but did not like taking medication: to him, if he were to take medication it would mean that there was something wrong with him. We saw a series of therapists including several who I know now should never have been allowed to practice. Nothing helped because he didn't want to do the hard work of healing or admit that there was something wrong with him. Instead, he blamed everything on me.

Mike verbally and sometimes physically assaulted me at home but not in public until the incident at the Golf train station. I thought about leaving but I had no support network. I had a professional job, two small children, a house in the suburbs that I had provided the down payment for and pets. The house was full of things with meaning to me. I was completely unprepared. No one had ever told me what domestic abuse was or how to get help. I had never talked about how to deal with a family member with a mental illness. I had no idea how to deal with what I wa facing. I tried everything to get help.

I called the local domestic violence shelter and described my situation to the volunteer who answered the phone only to be told that although my situation sounded dangerous, their shelter was full. Since it sounded like I had the financial means, the volunteer suggested I should look into finding a hotel or friend to stay with if things got too bad. The volunteer recommended I keep a bag packed in case I had to leave suddenly.

I called them back one other time, asking about joining a support group. This time I reached a staff member who told me there was a six-month waiting list for the group and they didn't take people with their own insurance since they could afford to get help on their own. This was before the American Affordable Care Act (ACA) when insurance coverage for mental health was not mandatory. It was also at a time when my Mike was scouring every bill that came into our house for evidence that I was unfaithful, so I was afraid to pay for something that my husband would question. I concluded that the shelter was never going to help me and never called again. I did make sure that I had all the things I needed to have to leave in a hurry in my purse or in my car.

Surviving on High Alert

As the years passed, my children made friends and became outstanding athletes. We joined a Unitarian Universalist Church, and I completed a graduate program, earning a Master of Business Administration

(MBA). I insulated myself from the abuse by focusing on work, my children, women's groups at the Church, and through online communities focused on books and needlework. My kids participated in every sport available but baseball. Both competed in national and international karate tournaments. I took them to most of their games and practices, volunteered to support their activities, and knew the other parents.

I told myself it wasn't that bad, denying the danger I was in. I hid how bad my situation was from others. I knew that I didn't want to flee and uproot my kids as I knew that fleeing would not guarantee my safety and it seemed so unfair that in order to be safe, I was expected to give up everything. I needed help getting Mike out of the house and could not find it.

Mike swore no one would ever believe me and that no one would let me keep the kids if he fought me in court. My experience with the domestic violence shelter convinced me this was true. Even the books that I read about domestic violence offered only two options: flee and leave everything behind or stay and try to change yourself and your attitude hoping that would reduce the abuse. Mike knew this. He goaded me, clearly seeing my despair and the position I was in. "No other man will ever want you," he sneered. "You'll be on your own, as I'll also have the kids and they'll never want to speak to you either."

As my son got older and larger, the amount of violence in our household increased as he started to fight with his father. The police got called to our house on a fairly regular basis. We tried counseling without success. Things continued to escalate with Mike becoming more violent and abusive when anything happened that highlighted my successes or when he was stressed. Finally, during an argument one evening in 2011, he hit me so hard on the side of my head that he knocked me out in front of our teenage children. When I came to, I left the house and tried to find somewhere to stay without success. I ended up creeping back into the house and sleeping on the couch. Mike left in the morning without saying anything to me.

Is This Supposed to Be Better?

I knew that the next time he got angry, he would kill me. I took the day off work and went to the police station and filed a report. In Illinois, it is up to the police and State's Attorney to pursue charges in a domestic violence case and in my case they did. Mike was arrested and charged with multiple counts of felony domestic battery and one non-domestic misdemeanor. I was granted an emergency restraining order, possession of the house, and full custody of our daughter—our son was already eighteen. I was left with everything that needed to be fed or cared for: two teenagers, two dogs, two cats, and a pair of geriatric hamsters. Mike moved in with his wealthy sister.

I was shocked to find out how difficult it was to get help of any kind. Church staff and lay leadership at the Church we attended refused to comply with the custody order and ignored the order of protection. No one from the congregation or staff called me and no one offered me or my kids any help or support. A few months later, Mike was invited to join the Church board.

At the time victim's services through the State's Attorney's office were only for victims of felonies or trial witnesses. When Mike's plea bargain agreement was accepted, I lost access to any support. The local domestic violence shelter had no programs for victims who didn't need emergency housing, so they had no services for me. I had never felt more alone, but at the same time I had never felt more free.

Growth and Healing

I adapted to life as a single parent and started to be an active participant in my community. I helped my kids maintain relationships with their father's extended family, continued to invite my ex-husband to family celebrations while providing a safe space in my home for my kids when they wanted or needed it. I continued to be part of some groups that Mike and I had belonged to together because I had friends there too. At our church, I continued to participate in activities where

I saw my friends and avoided activities that would bring me into contact with him.

In early 2019, I sought the help of a therapist. I was recovering from a back injury and experiencing flashbacks and panic attacks. I did a lot of research and was very selective, finally finding someone with experience with patients with PTSD and trauma who made me feel comfortable. My therapist made me feel safe and whole. He helped me make sense of things that had happened to me and to fully understand that I was none of the things that Mike had spent years telling me I was.

My therapist was especially proud of me when I started dating, and even that I kept dating after I was dumped by text. I ended up meeting my current boyfriend in January 2020. A big recovery milestone was that I was finally comfortable carrying a smaller purse, rather than having one with everything required should I need to run for help. By then I was even able to leave my house to walk my dogs without my phone in my hand.

System Fails Me Again

In late summer 2019, Mike was forced out of a job and became unbalanced. He reached out to me in ways that were concerning and made me feel unsafe. I found myself looking up information about obtaining orders of protection in Cook and Lake County Illinois, saving numbers into my phone, and checking the requirements for getting orders issued in one county served in another, again. It bothered me both that I was not better protected and that so little had changed.

I work as an engineer, solving complex problems and improving processes. I spend some time applying these skills to my situation and decided I had been failed by a system that was designed to fail me. I realized that my last opportunity to have someone force Mike to undergo a psychological evaluation and get treatment for his mental illness was when we were in the courtroom in 2011 after his arrest for domestic battery. No one at the time had asked if he had a previous diagnosis of mental illness. No one had talked about requiring an evaluation for mental illness. It had not even been considered. I am convinced that if the State's Attorney and the Judge had known about Mike's history of psychosis, they would not have accepted the plea agreement his attorney proposed and would not have allowed Mike to retain the ability to buy and own a gun by letting him plea to a non-domestic misdemeanor. I want to change that.

That fall I read *No Visible Bruises: What we Don't know about Domestic Violence Can Kill Us* by Rachel Louise Snyder. I couldn't believe that so much of my experience was captured in a book and that others agreed with the things that I found wrong with the existing responses to domestic violence. I firmly believe that our failure to recognize the danger of domestic violence and the connection between domestic violence, mass shootings, and domestic terrorism make us all less safe. I also love her assessment that we need to move past a shelter-based response to domestic violence. This response was based on the idea that victims were economically dependent on their abusers. We need to move to a system that keeps victims and their children in their homes and removes the abusers.

I started a two-pronged approach. First, I got myself in front of politicians and candidates to talk about making changes in the law, in court procedures, and in information provided on web sites to better serve victims of domestic violence like me. I also started talking to gun violence advocates about the fact that background checks won't work unless prosecutors and judges change how they address these cases. I have been more successful with the candidates and politicians than the gun violence advocates. There is a tendency to assume domestic violence victims are not white, educated, or middle class. In addition, people equate the fact that domestic violence advocates work very hard with effectiveness, but neither is entirely. The issue of domestic violence is universal: in fact, one in every four women will experience domestic violence in their lifetime. We do not provide victims with the tools they need to understand the danger they are in. And we fail to adequately support victims who are trying to find a way out to safety.

The biggest evidence of this failure is that so many advocates talk about victims who did everything right yet were still murdered by their abusers. To me, it should not be acceptable to say, "she did everything right, and he still found and killed her." If the end result is murder, then victims are not being provided with the right advice or the right options to protect themselves. Our system of response is not working; we need a new one.

Helping Her Recovery Through Advocacy

I ran for an open position on the Village Board of Trustees in 2021 and won. I am proud to support the police department that helped me and has adopted initiatives like adding a full-time social worker to their staff. I continue to advocate for change and hope to work with a new state senator and my current congressman on some legislative initiatives at the state and federal level.

Now that the COVID-19 pandemic is over, I am going to return to working in two areas that I am passionate about: making information for domestic violence victims available everywhere and training clergy in how to respond to domestic violence victims. Victims try to leave many times before they actually do so. It is very important that they have information available about tools that are available to support them.

I believe that there should be pamphlets in every public literature rack, business cards in every public restroom, and fliers in every doctor's office and in their waiting rooms. Now that pandemic restrictions have been lifted, I plan to go around and hand them out. I also think it is important for the type of people who victims confide in, like clergy, to be trained in how to respond to domestic violence victims. It is especially important to me that they know about the risk assessment models and can make them available to victims so that they can be fully aware of the risks that they face.

Back to Healing

I didn't accomplish all my goals in therapy; there are still things that I am afraid to do, but I feel whole. I am pleased that I can carry a smaller purse and I know that the only person I need to make happy is myself. I know that I am worthy of love and admiration. I know that it is worthwhile for me to work towards change.

After I won the election, I bought a red 2003 Ford Thunderbird convertible. When my kids heard about the car, they both told me that I was not only the best parent, I was also the coolest. I love to drive it and have taught my dogs to ride in it with the top down without trying to climb out. It feels good to no longer be afraid when I hit the gas on the tollway at night

Help Her RECOVER

In the midst of winter, I found there was, within me, an invincible summer. And that makes me happy.
For it says that no matter how hard the world pushes against me,
within me, there's something stronger – something better, pushing right back.

~ *Albert Camus*

Help Her RECOVER

By Amanda Willett

SELF DETERMINATION Principle 12, "I WORK TOWARD THE POSSIBILITY OF EFFECTIVENESS AND GROWTH IN MY OWN LIFE," embodies the idea that survivors of gender-based violence possess the agency and capacity to rebuild their lives on their own terms. It emphasizes the impor- tance of self-determination, where survivors are empowered to define their goals, make choices, and take actions that lead to personal growth and effectiveness. This principle encourages survivors to tap into their inner strength, set their aspirations, and work towards a future that reflects their desires and values. It recognizes that recovery is not just about healing from past trauma but also about forging a path towards a fulfilling and meaningful life. By fostering self-determination, we acknowledge that survivors are not defined solely by their past experiences; they have the potential to thrive and shape their own destinies.

We often hear about the problems faced by women attempting to flee gender-based violence, no support, no services, shelters are full, and waitlists are long, yet some people do overcome significant challenges and lead successful lives. Jenny is one of those people. Rather than flee and leave everything behind or stay and try to change herself and her attitude hoping that would reduce the abuse, Jenny decided there was a third option. She used her self-determination to take control of her destiny. Her desire to feel safe and to make change happen was greater than her desire to stay the same. She had been failed by a system that was designed to fail her, so Jenny decided to use this hurdle as fuel to make a difference.

Jenny Ross recounts her life, which initially seemed perfect but later turned into a nightmare due to her husband's mental health issues and abusive behavior. She highlights her determination to survive and protect her children. Her self-determination is evident as she navigates the challenges of seeking help and escaping an abusive marriage, even when the system fails her.

Over the years, Jenny adapts to life as a single parent, focuses on her career, and engages in various activities to build a support network. She undergoes therapy to heal from the trauma and regain her self-worth. Despite facing numerous obstacles, she persists in her efforts to effect change and improve the response to domestic violence, both in the legal system and the community.

Knowing firsthand our system of response to gender-based violence is not working and we need a new one, Jenny continues to advocate for change, she is determined to transform the system to better serve victims of domestic violence like her.

Self-determination is a combination of attitudes and abilities that lead people to set goals for themselves, and to take the initiative to reach these goals. Jenny's story reflects her resilience and determination to overcome adversity, ultimately finding a sense of freedom and fulfillment in her life. Her journey embodies the principle of self-determination, where she actively works toward effectiveness and growth, breaking free from the shackles of an abusive past. Jenny is proof that working toward the possibility of effectiveness and growth in our lives, is worth the journey. She has inspired me to continue my journey of advocating for survivors and building a trauma informed world.

SELF-DETERMINATION

Principle 12:
I WORK TOWARD THE POSSIBILITY OF EFFECTIVENESS
AND GROWTH IN MY OWN LIFE

How do I feel about change?
How can I turn change into opportunity?

Affirmation:

My determination fuels my progress, and I am making positive changes in my life.

Heart Opening Flow

Invitation: You may try this heart opening practice from a seated or standing position. I invite you on an inhale breath to lift your arms up to the sky. Notice the fortitude of your body, the container it holds for the range of your emotions. Notice your growth as you and stretch and lengthen through your spine, up to your fingertips. When you feel ready, draw your palms together overhead, if that is available to you. On the exhale, I invite you to lower your arms and draw them in towards your heart space. You can choose to repeat this practice for as long as you wish. Finishing with palms together in prayer pose, consider all the infinite possibilities available to you. You are worthy of everything your heart desires.

Mindful Focusing Meditation: Even if I make mistakes while trying, I will still try my best every time because eventually, I will succeed! Mistakes are how I learn. Whatever happens, I'll handle it. I have grit and I won't quit.

Find a quiet and comfortable place to sit or lie down. Close your eyes and take a few deep breaths to center yourself.

Setting Your Intention:

Start by setting your intention for this meditation. Say to yourself, "I am here to connect with my inner determination and embrace positive changes in my life."

Focus on Your Breath:

Pay attention to your breath. Feel the natural rhythm of your breath as you inhale and exhale. Let your breath be a source of calm and presence.

Body Scan:

Take a moment to scan your body from head to toe. Notice any areas of tension or discomfort. As you breathe, imagine sending a soothing, warm light to these areas, allowing them to relax.

Affirmation Repetition:

Repeat the affirmation silently or out loud: "My determination fuels my progress, and I am making positive changes in my life." Visualize each word of the affirmation as you say it.

Visualize Your Goals:

Envision the positive changes you want to make in your life. See them clearly in your mind's eye. Imagine yourself taking steps toward these goals with determination and confidence.

Connect with Your Inner Determination:

Reflect on times when you've demonstrated determination and achieved positive outcomes in the past. Feel the strength and resilience within you that led to those achievements.

Breathing in Determination:

As you continue to breathe, imagine that with each inhale, you are drawing in a powerful energy of determination. Feel it filling your entire being, invigorating you with purpose.

Let Go of Limiting Beliefs:

Identify any limiting beliefs or self-doubt that may be holding you back. Acknowledge these thoughts without judgment, and then release them with each exhale.

Embrace Change:

Embrace the idea that change is a natural part of life and personal growth. Welcome change as an opportunity for positive transformation.

Gratitude:

Take a moment to express gratitude for your determination and the progress you've already made in your life. Recognize your own resilience.

Closing:

Gently return your focus to your breath. Feel the rise and fall of your chest with each breath. When you're ready, slowly open your eyes.

Carry the Determination:

As you go about your day, carry the sense of determination and the affirmation with you. Whenever you face challenges or opportunities for positive change, remind yourself of your inner strength and commitment.

This meditation can help you tap into your inner determi- nation, empower positive changes, and reinforce your belief in your ability to make progress in your life. Practice it regularly to support your journey of self-determination and growth.

SPEAK OUT

ESTHER ENYOLU

Esther Enyolu is the Executive Director of Women Multicultural Resource and Counselling Centre of Durham (WMRCC). She is a dynamic leader on the issues of gender-based violence, human rights, diversity, equity, inclusion, and social justice. She believes in creating a safe environment that is free of all forms of violence and oppression.

Esther works with different universities and colleges, including community organizations on issues of gender-based violence and to promote entrepreneurship for women from diverse backgrounds through the charitable organization that she has led for over thirty years. She lives with family in both Simcoe County and Durham Region in Ontario, Canada. She says this has widen her knowledge on issues that impact the lives of members in both areas.

SUPPORTING AND EMPOWERING WOMEN AND CHILDREN WITH LIVED EXPERIENCES OF VIOLENCE AND ABUSE

By
Esther Enyolu

"We want to turn victims into survivors and survivors into thrivers".

Tarana Burke

At age twenty, I moved to Canada from Nigeria to join my fiancé. I arrived on a Saturday and by Monday morning I registered for the Sociology/Anthropology program at Carleton University in Ottawa. I went back in the evening to start my course. Initially, I had planned to study nursing, as I was fantasizing becoming a nurse when I was in high school but later changed my mind.

My mother used to say that she wanted my immediate younger brother to become a medical doctor and me to become a nurse so we could provide good medical care to her and our dad when they get old and are probably dealing with health-related challenges associated with old age. As I got older, I realized that the health care field was not my calling. I switched my direction from pursuing nursing to social sciences to help women, youth, and children dealing with issues of violence and abuse. It seems to me this was where I could do the best in the world. This is how I could serve my communities.

I grew up in a family which had a great responsibility to others. My parents were quite respected due to their commitments in supporting people navigating their marital and other life challenges. They gave selflessly of their time, even though it was a community support work for them as they both had their professional jobs. I was intrigued; I also noticed that I was good with people, just like my parents. I realized seeing my parents handling cases of spouses dealing with personal and family issues in Nigeria also impacted my decision to go into the social services/social work field. People came to see my parents, particularly my mother, when they had family issues. Whenever the couples or individuals (most of these individuals were women) came to our home for such purpose, my parents would order my siblings and I to leave because they did not want us to be around to hear the stories. I witnessed my parents' influence from other side of the doors. The couples and individuals supported often came back to thank them with gifts or to testify that things had gotten better.

I was aware of the different types of family structures in various countries. As a woman who was once a newcomer, I could only imagine how challenging and isolating it must have been for some newcomers and immigrant women. More especially those who have no family support network and are experiencing intimate partner violence or gender-based violence would be coping.

Though I had a supportive partner assisting me to transition to a new culture and environment, it was still challenging for me dealing with "culture shock" as a new immigrant. I began asking myself if I was going through the culture shock with all the support, what about women who came here not having any support network, how about those with no status in Canada, or those who found themselves in an abusive situation, especially if they are living with disabilities or a language barrier? This contributed to my decision to move into social service field to support them, including the following factors:

- Following my parents' footsteps of supporting the community
- Being exposed to media interview of women who experienced intimate-partner violence on a Superbowl weekend.

Those women complained about being victims of intimate-partner violence in the past when the team their spouses were supporting lost the game. Some were stating they already booked a hotel to lodge in at that weekend. I saw all those photos of women on TV with visible signs of violence and trauma: black and red eyes, bruises, being injured, some had sustained due to Superbowl game weekends. They were suggesting to other women who might be in the same predicament to stay in hotels or with family members. I could not believe it. Why would women suffer because a team lost a game? I was astounded.

I could see that when individuals internalize and normalize intimate partner violence, it becomes "a culture" of condoning. A man feels he owns and is entitled to treat his partner as he wants, that becomes a serious issue. Also, when some in-laws live with the couple, they can be part of the problem or part of the solution. That is, they can condemn or condone the abusive behaviour. In some situations, when the problem is normalized, the in-laws might be involved in abusing the woman. They become part of the problem. They tend to have high expectation of the woman which could lead to subjecting her to further abuse.

I was aware that abuse and violence occur in all cultures, races, communities, sexualities, faith communities and societies. At the time I moved to Durham Region of Ontario, Canada, which was not at all diverse in the 90s. I became part of a community study conducting focus group sessions and gathering data about newcomers and immigrant women's experience of gender-based violence and level of their satisfaction with the services received.

This study was commissioned by Dr. Barbara Rahder and Associates through a grant from the Ontario Government. I was recruited as an analyst to work with the late Kay Blair, the Executive Director of the Community Micro Skills Development Center. A need assessment study was conducted with women experiencing intimate-partner violence in four Ontario counties: Durham Region, Northumberland, Lindsay, and Peterborough.

There was no multicultural organization back then supporting newcomers and women from diverse backgrounds with lived experiences of violence in Durham Region. Having worked in Toronto where such organizations existed, I wanted to do something in Durham Region. In a very short time, we had over thirty women ready to participate in the focus group sessions.

We held the focus group sessions on Saturdays. We collected and collated data on their lived experiences. The information we collected were used for the report we shared with the community and funding ministry. A few consultation sessions were also held with different organizations and institutions to share the findings and recommendations. At the conclusion of the study, we maintained contact with the women who participated and continued to support them. The women unequivocally recommended that a counselling center and shelter to focus on newcomers, immigrant, and racialized women were needed.

Although the women wanted a shelter, we did not move on with such a recommendation as a counselling centre was the more feasible option. We recruited some of the women who participated in the focus group to become the first board of directors, and an organization was born, Women's Rights Action Coalition of Durham. The name of the organization was later changed to Women's Multicultural Resource and Counselling Centre of Durham (WMRCC) in 2003. We also founded a group called "Durham WATCH" which stands for Women's Action Towards CHANGE.

Our initial challenge was a lack of the funding to run the organization, but, persistence, resilience, commitment and passion has enabled WMRCC to continue to support many newcomers, immigrants, and women from diverse communities who need such services and programs to heal from experiences of trauma. WMRCC is a trauma informed care healing place for women of all ages, youth, and children. The organization also supports women in business and is a centre for Worker Cooperative Development for Women in Ontario, Canada. We have dealt with numerous cases and supported many individuals in the community to break the barriers of navigating social service systems.

One of the challenging cases we have dealt with was a newcomer woman who migrated to join her spouse. When she arrived, he would not allow her to go anywhere without him accompanying her. He would not let her to speak to her family or the neighbors. She was quite isolated and in a severe abusive relationship.

There was a language barrier, she was not aware about Canadian culture, nor did she know where to turn for help. All this kept her isolated, and a prisoner in her own home. One day as they returned from an outing, a male neighbour said hello to them, and she reciprocated. When they got inside the house, her husband started yelling at her, beating, kicking, and shoving her around. He alleged she was having a relationship with the man and proceeded to stab her.

The neighbors heard her screaming and called emergency services. Miraculously, she survived the attack; however, her injuries were so severe that she was hospitalized for several months. Doctors and nurses were amazed she survived such a serious attack. WMRCC supported her to deal with the trauma after she got out of the hospital. We also got her help through other community services.

As service providers, we have been seeing and dealing with many similar stories. And for each woman, we step in and offer practical support. We work with clienteles from a feminist, anti-racist, and anti-oppression perspective. It is an intersectional approach of gender-based violence and other forms of oppressions. That is, we work with service users from "gender-based plus" lens or analysis. While working with them on their lived experiences of violence, we tend not to overlook the impact of systemic issues based on their social locations. Social locations include but are not limited to race, ethnicity, sexuality, intellectual and physical disabilities, language, gender expressions, age, immigration status, economic status, class and caste, education or literacy level, religion, health condition or geographical area. We look at all these intersecting factors as they create barriers and inequities to social and economic opportunities that contributes to poor mental health and social well-being.

We must use such lens in order to provide effective and appropriate culturally responsive services and programs to the communities we serve. For instance, a Black woman, an Indigenous woman, or a racialized woman coming to us is most likely to be dealing with lived experiences of violence/inter-generational trauma and perhaps also lived experiences of systemic racism and discrimination.

Also, we are not relegating their lived experiences related to sexuality, ability, age or religion. Muslim women face Islamophobia in addition to lived experiences of discrimination based on class, caste system, ethnicities, and language. Sexual diverse women and youth face homophobia. Women and youth living with disabilities face ableism. Women in abusive situations are already vulnerable and such vulnerability puts them in a predicament situation. Colonialism, neo-colonialism, and patriarchal culture have negative impacts in the lives of most newcomers, immigrants, and racialized communities.

I am doing this work because I want to support others, being an immigrant woman myself. I know how difficult it was back then adjusting to a new culture and environment despite all the support I was getting from my spouse and others. Imagine these women going through settlement and adjustment issues with abuse and violence on top of it, and not having any family support network. The organization that I work for has helped thousands of women, youth, and children in the community for 3 decades.

So many women, youth, and children have cried on my shoulder and the shoulders of my team members and colleagues. WMRCC's aim is to help them to overcome the trauma they have experienced. To help them understand that whatever they have experienced was not their fault and that they are not alone as many community members are in the same situation. The need not to suffer in silence. For them not be ashamed or blame themselves for the violence or abuse they suffered. They are never alone; it can happen to anyone irrespective of their social status or social location.

WMRCC of Durham exists to support them to know that when they feel the world is against them or that everyone has turned their backs on them, we are a family and one of the community support services they can lean on for support. We are here to support; listen, empower them to know that help is only a phone call away. We provide non-judgemental services. We help them with legal issues, housing, immigration issues for those who migrated with refugee status or non-status individuals, employment and skills development, entrepreneurship, micro skills, self-empowerment workshops, support group sessions, civic engagement, networking, mentorship, and many more. We advocate and also support them with the process of obtaining immigration status in Canada through referral to immigration lawyers. Not to talk about child custody and access issues that can be draining to these women. The process seems to be too long and if a woman does not qualify for "legal aid certificate" it makes the matter worse for her.

Some of the families coming to us are greatly impoverished; we find resources for them like food banks, food vouchers, and other community services that support with food delivering and weekly groceries. Even though these issues existed before the COVID-19 pandemic, we have observed the escalation during and after the pandemic, especially as inflation continues to rise daily. Individual cases are never straightforward; there are many complexities that must not be ignored as that is the only way we can achieve equity and social justice.

As a great writer, Audre Lorde said, "there is no such thing as a single-issue struggle because we do not live single-issue lives." We should make issues patterning to other people our own struggle because that is the only way we can achieve equity and social justice.

Social housing is a big challenge, we are dealing with severe housing crisis, and it is hurting majority of our clienteles. Housing is unaffordable. It is creating serious homelessness issues in various communities. But irrespective of these challenges, it is my passion to engage in this work because there is a lot of need in the community. So, we all need to get out of our comfort zone to continue to work tirelessly in the community for the change that we need to see.

I am dedicating this article to my parents, people who have contributed to my growth and well-being, my spouse and children, my colleagues and team in the front-line supporting survivors of violence and abuse, women of all ages, youth and children who turn to us for support. It takes the entire community to eradicate violence against women and children, as well as building a safe community that has zero tolerance on issues of gender-based violence and other forms of oppressions. We cannot deal with one issue without its' intersectionality to other issues that affect humanity.

Help Her RECOVER

We're all just walking
each other home.

~ *Ram Dass*

Help Her RECOVER

By Amanda Willett

"COMMUNITY Principle 13: I AM SURROUNDED WITH A CIRCLE OF LIGHT AND LOVE" underscores the vital role of a supportive community in the recovery process from gender-based violence. It emphasizes that survivors should not bear the burden alone but should be enveloped by a network of understanding and compassionate individuals who provide emotional, psychological, and practical assistance. This principle recognizes that healing is not solely an individual journey but a collective effort where the survivor is embraced by a circle of people who offer love, empathy, and a safe space for vulnerability. Community support serves as a source of strength, reinforcing the survivor's worth and providing the affirmation needed to rebuild a sense of self and trust in others. Ultimately, it highlights the transformative power of community solidarity in the path towards recovery and resilience.

Esther Enyolu, the Executive Director of the Women's Multicultural Centre of Durham, shares a powerful chapter in the book emphasizing the indispensable role of a supportive community in the recovery journey from gender-based violence. Esther's chapter unfolds with her personal journey as an immigrant woman from Nigeria, driven by a passion to support women, youth, and children dealing with issues of violence and abuse. Influenced by her parents' commitment to community support, she transitioned from nursing aspirations to the social services field, where she felt she could make the most significant impact. Her upbringing, witnessing her parents' compassionate intervention in cases of marital challenges in Nigeria, further fueled her dedication to social service.

As a newcomer herself, Esther experienced the challenges of cultural adjustment and realized the added difficulties faced by immigrant women dealing with intimate partner violence. Her commitment to addressing these challenges led her to initiate a community study in Durham Region, revealing the lack of multicultural organizations supporting women with lived experiences of violence. This gap prompted the establishment of the Women's Multicultural Resource and Counselling Centre of Durham (WMRCC), previously known as the Women's Action Coalition of Durham.

Esther delves into the complexities of gender-based violence, recognizing its existence across cultures, races, and communities. She shares compelling stories, including a poignant case of a newcomer woman subjected to severe abuse, highlighting the intersectional approach of WMRCC—addressing gender-based violence alongside other forms of oppression.

The chapter emphasizes the critical importance of a trauma-informed care approach, creating a healing space for women, youth, and children. WMRCC, under Esther Enyolu's leadership, not only supports survivors through counseling but also addresses systemic issues based on social locations such as race, ethnicity, disability, and more.

Esther advocates for a comprehensive lens, incorporating an intersectional approach to understand and address the diverse barriers and inequities faced by survivors. The organization provides a range of services, from legal support and housing assistance to employment development and entrepreneurship programs.

The narrative takes a global perspective, acknowledging the impacts of colonialism, neo-colonialism, and patriarchal culture on newcomers, immigrants, and racialized communities. Enyolu's dedication stems from her personal experience as an immigrant woman and a firm belief in the power of community support.

In conclusion, Esther's chapter is a testament to the tireless efforts of WMRCC in supporting survivors and advocating for equity and social justice. It echoes the principle that collective action within a supportive community is essential to eradicating gender-based violence and building a safe environment with zero tolerance for oppression. The chapter serves as a beacon of hope, encouraging readers to step out of their comfort zones and actively contribute to positive change in their communities.

COMMUNITY

Principle 13:
I AM SURROUNDED WITH A CIRCLE
OF LIGHT AND LOVE

Explore the idea of reciprocity in your relationships. How can you give and receive support, kindness, and love within your circle of light and love?

Affirmation:

In the presence of light makers, I am reminded of my own potential for greatness.

Star Yoga Pose - (Utthita Tadasana)

Stand in mountain pose (tadasana) with your feet about hips width distance apart and your back tall., I invite you to step your feet out wide and extend your arms up toward the sky. Press down through your heels and straighten your legs fully. Draw your knees up by engaging your thigh muscles and keep your feet solidly grounded through the floor. Press evenly through all corners of the feet. With your legs wide apart and your feet firmly planted in the earth, allow yourself to receive the energy of love, joy and support. You might explore a "V" shape or "X" with your arms and legs, gaze up to the sky, add a little backbend and finish with a forward fold or bow to the ground.

Breathe and imagine you are a big star in the sky, part of a beautiful constellation, a web of stars. Once you are in the pose, take 4-8 deep breaths while maintaining the posture to really get the full effect. Please get curious, explore and do what feels accessible and supportive in your body.

Mindful Focusing Meditation:

Practicing mindfulness within a supportive community can be a powerful way to tap into your own potential and be inspired by others. Here's a mindful meditation practice for the theme of community and recognizing your potential for greatness:

Duration: 10-15 minutes (adjust as needed)

Instructions:

1. **Find a Comfortable Space:** Begin by finding a quiet and comfortable place where you can sit or lie down. Ensure that you won't be disturbed during your meditation.
2. **Relaxation:** Take a few deep breaths to settle into the present moment. With each exhale, let go of any tension in your body, and allow yourself to relax.
3. **Setting the Intention:** Set your intention for this meditation by recognizing that you are part of a supportive community. You are surrounded by individuals who inspire and uplift you, and you, too, have the potential for greatness.
4. **Focus on Breath:** Bring your attention to your breath. Notice the natural rhythm of your breath, the rise and fall of your chest or the sensation of the breath at your nostrils.
5. **Visualize a Circle of Light:** Imagine yourself sitting at the center of a beautiful circle of light. This light represents the collective wisdom, love, and support of your community. Visualize this light shining brightly around you.

6. **Connecting with Others:** In your mind's eye, see the individuals in your community who inspire you and whom you admire. These can be friends, mentors, family members, or anyone who has had a positive impact on your life.

7. **Share in Their Light:** Imagine each of these individuals as radiant sources of light within the circle. See their light shining brightly, filling the space around you. Feel their positive energy, wisdom, and love.

8. **Recognize Your Potential:** As you bask in the collective light of your community, reflect on your own potential for greatness. Acknowledge that you, too, possess unique qualities, talents, and potential waiting to be realized.

9. **Affirmations:** Silently repeat positive affirmations that resonate with you, such as: "I am surrounded by a supportive community." I am inspired by the greatness of others." "I recognize my own potential for greatness."

10. **Embrace Inspiration:** As you continue to breathe mindfully, allow the inspiration and positive energy from your community to flow into you. Feel it filling your heart and mind with motivation and confidence.

11. **Visualize Your Light:** Visualize your own inner light growing brighter within the circle. Imagine it expanding and radiating outwards, representing your unique potential.

12. **Deepen the Connection:** Take a few moments to deepen your connection with your community and your own potential. Feel the sense of belonging and support that surrounds you.

13. **Gratitude:** Before concluding the practice, express gratitude for the community that uplifts and inspires you, and for the potential within yourself.

14. **Return to the Present:** Gently open your eyes if they were closed, and sit quietly for a moment, carrying this sense of connection and potential with you as you go about your day.

This meditation practice can help you tap into the inspiration and support of your community while recognizing and nurturing your own potential for greatness. You can return to this practice whenever you wish to connect with your community and embrace your inner potential.

By Sarah Lewis

DIVINE WOMAN

**(spoken word poetry is to be read aloud–
please refer to QR code to hear author read poem)**

divine woman, rest your weary eyes and worries
set them aside woman
for an older version of yourself to worry about
you are welcome to step off the pedestal they have placed
you on
breathe
release the tension in your shoulders, neck back
the battles will always be there, so unclench your fists
place hands in prayer pose
and thank yourself for how hard you have worked to get
here to this moment
divine woman
super kind woman, kinda woman who doesn't take too
kind to people who tell her to be kind and neat and smile
please, when she grinds in these capitalist streets so she can
feed her babies

who is working so hard to love herself after decades of
unsolicited advice woman
who is called every objectifying name in the book
but returns the book to its owner, has never been much of a
fiction reader woman
loud woman
not a femme bot, plot twist, and twerk and bend for you
fantasy, living to appease the male gaze, lying naked underneath willow tree, docile, sweet, submissive, whispering
never yelling
cooking
never burning
bridges
expected to do it all woman
but she doesn't feel full off these capitalist calories
she has a hunger for community, for connection
was born in a system that fed her lies
she's is a more than enough woman
they gave her a manual on how to be a good real woman,
yet they want to pluck and wax off all her real-ness, put her
on a diet, tone her voice down
but she knows she's a goddess, and no goddess would dare
remove parts of herself, make herself less goddess like
divine woman
beautiful mind woman
not a forget me not, but a woman you remember
she is the whole fire, not just the embers kind of woman
her body's cells are derived from precolonial contact, cannot be owned or told what to do, her parts are not a refer-
ence point for abuse or patriarchal profit, she's a prophet of
poetry of self-love of raging against the system

that covers her breast as if it exposed its secrets
makes them uncomfortable seeing it in a baby's mouth, but not if it's wrapped in Victoria's Secret
"wants to see me nude but not too much, and not with additional baggage or fat, but only if it sits on my hips, chest or ass "
And divine woman knows that to heal from the patriarchal melting pot, is to get out of the pot, is to stir the pot, knows that it is not enough to say sorry or not all men, it is to unlearn sexism rooted in colonialism, is to provide reparations
is to love our women
to respect all women, that's trans women, disabled women, gay women, straight women, fat women, skinny women, loud women, quiet women, masculine women, sexual women, asexual women, not your women, black women, indigenous women,
to acknowledge your existence is because of women
this is for the women who want to have kids, the women who dont, the married women, the women who won't, the poly women, working moms, moms that don't work, the women who wear makeup, and the ones that have made up their minds that their freckles are too fine to cover, not hard to find woman because she's listening to this poem right now, I see you divine woman
and so please, stop placing her on a pedestal
she will always desecrate it, set it to flame
she exists to exist, and doesn't need to make it pretty
she isn't merely a vibe, but a whole frequency that radiates love, magic, womanhood and divinity

RESOURCES

These resources cover a range of support services and organizations that can be invaluable for survivors and those looking to learn more about gender-based violence:

Community Resources and Helplines: Providing immediate help and crisis support.

National Domestic Violence Hotline: Assaulted Women's Helpline
Toll-free: 1-866-863-0511 (multilingual services available) Toll-free TTY: Phone: 1-800-799-SAFE (7233) or #SAFE (#7233) on your Bell, Rogers, Fido or Telus mobile phone.

Fem'aide Helpline (French only)
Telephone: 1-877-336-2433 (services available in French only)
TTY: 1-866-860-7082

Centre d'aide aux victimes d'actes criminels (CAVAC)
Telephone: 1 866 LE CAVAC (1-866-532-2822)
Website: https://cavac.qc.ca/en/

Talk4Healing (Helpline for Indigenous Women)
Toll-free: 1-855-554-4325 (multilingual services available)   Prince Edward Island
Website: www.thehotline.org
Text: Text "LOVEIS" to 1-866-331-9474

Ontario Coalition of Rape Crisis Centres
Website: https://sexualassaultsupport.ca/

RAINN (Rape, Abuse & Incest National Network):
Website: www.rainn.org

National Sexual Assault Hotline: 1-800-656-HOPE (4673)

National Network to End Domestic Violence (NNEDV):
Website: www.nnedv.org

Futures Without Violence:
Website: www.futureswithoutviolence.org

Love Is Respect (for teen dating violence):
Website: www.loveisrespect.org
Phone: 1-866-331-9474
Text: Text "LOVEIS" to 22522

National Coalition Against Domestic Violence (NCADV):
Website: www.ncadv.org

National Organization for Victim Assistance (NOVA):
Website: www.trynova.org

The Women's Multicultural Resource and Counselling Centre of Durham Region is dedicated to providing specialized counselling and support to women of all ages and their families, from diverse backgrounds, to eradicate violence, to rebuild their lives, and to enable them to become contributing and valued members of society. Website: https://wmrcc.org/

Canada:
Ending Violence Association of Canada: *https://endingviolencecanada.org/*

USA:
National Sexual Violence Resource Center: *https://www.nsvrc.org/find-help*
Victim Connect Resource Center: *https://victimconnect.org/resources/national-hotlines/*

United Kingdom:
National Health Service: *https://www.nhs.uk/live-well/sexual-health/help-after-rape-and-sexual-assault/*
24/7 Rape and Sexual Abuse Support: *https://247sexualabusesupport.org.uk/*

Joyful Heart Foundation:
Website: www.joyfulheartfoundation.org

Men Can Stop Rape:
Website: www.mencanstoprape.org
1in6 (support for male survivors of sexual assault):
Website: www.1in6.org

Malawi, Africa:
The Coalition for the Empowerment of Women and Girls (CEWAG) is a NGO operating in Malawi, aiming to ensure that women and girls are able to enjoy their rights and participate fully in public affairs. Established in 2016, CEWAG provides training to empower girls and young women with skills, and conducts community campaigns to raise awareness and change perspectives and beliefs that are harmful to girls and young women. The organisation also engages traditional leaders as agents for change, through lobbying and advocacy efforts.
info@cewagmw.org, https://www.facebook.com/CEWAGMalawi/

JASS HIV/AIDS work started in 2006 in Malawi resulting in the "Our Bodies Our Lives" campaign in 2012, a movement that aimed at improving access to safer anti-retroviral medication and quality health care for women living with HIV. https://justassociates.org/jass_map_data/malawi/

National Human Trafficking Hotline:
Website: humantraffickinghotline.org
Phone: 1-888-373-7888
Text: Text "HELP" or "INFO" to 233733

Women's Shelters and Resources:
https://www.oaith.ca/ - OAITH stands for the "Ontario Association of Interval & Transition Houses." It is a nonprofit organization based in Ontario, Canada, that focuses on supporting and advocating for shelters and services for women and children who have experienced gender-based violence, including domestic violence and intimate partner violence.

Online Directories: Websites like **DomesticShelters.org, Women Shelters.org, https://sheltersafe.ca/, and https://endvaw.ca/** offer resources, directories of women's shelters and domestic violence services by state and city.

Educational Resources:

GBV Resource Collective - They exist to bridge the gap between survivors of violence and the organizations that provide support. Through their website they share targeted resources, education, and advocacy from the Gender-Based Violence Sector. Through their Help Portal, survivors can pull curated resources for their specific needs. https://gbvresourcecollective.ca/

Coursera and edX - These online learning platforms offer courses on topics related to gender-based violence, trauma, and recovery. Search for courses on these platforms to find relevant educational materials. https://www.coursera.org/learn/gender-based-violence

Books: These books cover various aspects of trauma recovery and gender-based violence, so it's important to choose the ones that resonate most with your specific interests and needs.

"The Courage to Heal: A Guide for Women Survivors of Child Sexual Abuse" was published by Harper & Row in 1988. It was authored by Ellen Bass and Laura Davis and has been an influential resource for survivors of child sexual abuse seeking support and healing.

"The Sexual Healing Journey: A Guide for Survivors of Sexual Abuse" by Wendy Maltz was published by HarperOne in 2011. This book offers a holistic approach to healing from sexual abuse and provides exercises and techniques for recovery.

"Why Does He Do That? Inside the Minds of Angry and Controlling Men" by Lundy Bancroft was published by Berkley Books, an imprint of Penguin Group, in 2002. - Lundy Bancroft, a leading expert on abusive relationships, explores the mindset of abusive men and offers insights for survivors and those trying to help them.

"Healing from Hidden Abuse: A Journey Through the Stages of Recovery from Psychological Abuse" by Shannon Thomas was published by Scid Society Press in 2016. This book is focused on psychological abuse, this book guides survivors through the recovery process and provides tools for healing.

"I Left My Toxic Relationship – Now What?: The Step-by-Step Guide to Starting over and Living on Your Own" by Heather Kent was published by CreateSpace Independent Publishing Platform on October 18, 2016.

You've already taken the first big step in starting your new life, but now what? If you are looking for a road map for independence with active steps to take in order to get there, *I Left My Toxic Relationship – Now What?* is for you.

Heal from Your Narcissist Ex: The Ultimate Guide to Finding Safety and Sanity by Heather Kent was published by Difference Press on August 23, 2016.

In Heal from Your Narcissist Ex, #1 bestselling author, psychotherapist, and educator, Heather Kent, teaches you the framework that will get you from fear of the phone ringing to having the safe and independent freedom you dream of.

"The Body Keeps the Score: Brain, Mind, and Body in the Healing of Trauma" by Bessel van der Kolk was published by Viking on September 25, 2014. - This book explores how trauma affects the body and mind and provides insights into the recovery process.

"No Visible Bruises: What We Don't Know About Domestic Violence Can Kill Us" by Rachel Louise Snyder was published by Bloomsbury Publishing on May 14, 2019. - Snyder's book delves into the often-hidden epidemic of domestic violence and offers a compassionate and comprehensive look at the issue.

"I Am Malala: The Girl Who Stood Up for Education and Was Shot by the Taliban" by Malala Yousafzai was published by Little, Brown and Company on October 8th, 2013. - Malala's inspiring memoir tells her story of survival and her fight for girls' education.

"Not That Bad: Dispatches from Rape Culture" edited by Roxane Gay was published by Harper Perennial on May 1st, 2018. - A collection of essays that explores various aspects of rape culture and the impact it has on survivors.

Complex PTSD: From Surviving to Thriving: A Guide and Map for Recovering from Childhood Trauma, by Pete Walker was published by Azure Coyote Books in 2013. This is a valuable resource for individuals who have experienced complex trauma and for mental health professionals working with trauma survivors. It offers a compassionate and comprehensive approach to healing from the long-lasting effects of childhood trauma, providing hope and guidance for moving from survival to a place of thriving and greater emotional well-being.

The Abandonment Recovery Workbook: Guidance through the Five Stages of Healing from Abandonment, Heartbreak, and Loss, by Susan Anderson was published by New World Library in August 2016.

This book is for anyone dealing with the emotional aftermath of abandonment, heartbreak, or loss. It offers a structured and compassionate approach to healing, providing readers with the tools they need to work through their pain, gain self-awareness, and ultimately move toward a place of emotional well-being and resilience.

The Dance of Anger: A Woman's Guide to Changing the Patterns of Intimate Relationships, by Harriet Lerner was published by Harper & Row in 1985. A renowned self-help book that explores the dynamics of anger within intimate relationships, with a particular focus on women's experiences. The book provides valuable insights and guidance on how women can effectively deal with and transform the patterns of anger in their relationships.

"Why Does He Do That?: Inside the Minds of Angry and Controlling Men" by Lundy Bancroft was published by Berkley Books in September 2002.

Lundy Bancroft, a renowned expert on domestic abuse, delves into the mindset of abusive men and offers insights into their behavior.

"Trauma and Recovery: The Aftermath of Violence - From Domestic Abuse to Political Terror" by Judith Herman was published by Basic Books and first released in 1992.

Dr. Judith Herman explores the psychological and emotional impact of trauma, including gender-based violence, and offers a framework for recovery.

"I Can't Get Over It: A Handbook for Trauma Survivors" by Aphrodite T. Matsakis was published by New Harbinger Publications, and the first edition was released in 1992.

This book provides practical advice and coping strategies for trauma survivors dealing with the long-term effects of trauma.

"The Verbally Abusive Relationship: How to Recognize It and How to Respond" by Patricia Evans was published by Adams Media, and the first edition was released in 1992.

Focusing on verbal abuse, this book helps readers identify and respond to abusive behaviors in relationships.

"The Trauma of Everyday Life" by Mark Epstein was published by Penguin Press and was first published in 2013.

While not specific to gender-based violence, this book explores the role of trauma in everyday life and how mindfulness and Buddhism can aid in healing.

Documentaries:

"The Hunting Ground" - This documentary focuses on sexual assault on college campuses in the United States and the survivors who are fighting for justice.

"Audrie & Daisy" - The film follows the stories of two teenage girls who experienced sexual assault and the impact it had on their lives.

"Private Violence" - This documentary sheds light on domestic violence and the often-overlooked issue of intimate partner violence.

"Telling Amy's Story" - A documentary that tells the story of Amy Homan-McGee, a domestic violence victim, and the efforts to prevent such tragedies.

"**The Invisible War**" - This film addresses sexual assault in the U.S. military and the struggles survivors face in seeking justice.

Legal Aid and Advocacy Organizations:

International Organizations:

UN Women (www.unwomen.org) - UN Women is the United Nations entity dedicated to gender equality and the empowerment of women. They work globally to support survivors and advocate for policies and laws that address gender-based violence.

Amnesty International (www.amnesty.org) - Amnesty International works to protect and promote human rights worldwide, including advocating for the rights and safety of survivors of gender-based violence.

Global Rights for Women (www.globalrightsforwomen.org) - This organization works to promote international women's rights, including legal advocacy and support for survivors.

U.S. Organizations:

Legal Momentum (www.legalmomentum.org) - Legal Momentum is a U.S. legal defense and education fund dedicated to advancing the rights of women and girls. They provide legal assistance and advocacy on various gender-based violence issues.

National Women's Law Center (www.nwlc.org) - The National Women's Law Center focuses on women's rights and gender justice, including legal advocacy for survivors of gender-based violence.

Futures Without Violence (www.futureswithoutviolence.org) - Futures Without Violence works to end violence against women and children and provides resources, including legal support, for survivors.

RAINN (Rape, Abuse & Incest National Network) (www.rainn.org) - RAINN offers a National Sexual Assault Hotline and provides legal information and resources for survivors of sexual violence in the United States.

Canadian Organizations:

Canadian Network of Women's Shelters and Transition Houses (www.endvaw.ca) - This network advocates for women's shelters and transition houses across Canada and provides resources for survivors of domestic violence.

Canadian Association of Elizabeth Fry Societies (www.caefs.ca) - The association works with and for women involved with the criminal justice system, including those who have experienced gender-based violence.

Legal Aid Canada (www.legalaid.ca) - Legal Aid Canada provides legal assistance to low-income individuals, including survivors of gender-based violence who may require legal representation.

Women's Legal Education and Action Fund (LEAF) (www.leaf.ca) - LEAF is a Canadian organization that works to advance the equality of women and girls through litigation, law reform, and public education.

Please note that the availability of services and programs may vary among organizations, and it's essential to contact these organizations directly or visit their websites for specific information on the legal assistance and advocacy they provide for survivors of gender-based violence.

Counseling and Therapy Services:

Finding a therapist or counselor experienced in working with survivors of trauma and gender-based violence is crucial for the healing process. Here is a list of international resources and directories that can help you find qualified professionals:

Rituals for Recovery https://ritualsforrecovery.com/help-her-recover-services

Provides personalized care, through therapy, coaching and counselling for survivors of complex trauma. Their team of licensed practitioners offer free and sliding scale trauma focused care and compassionate support services for those recovering from stress, anxiety, depression, PTSD, grief and loss, physical illness, and various forms of complex trauma such as, sexual assault, narcissistic abuse, bullying, and gender-based violence.

Psychology Today (www.psychologytoday.com) or www.psychology-today.com/ca): Psychology Today's directory allows you to search for therapists by location, specialty, and insurance. Many therapists list their experience in trauma and gender-based violence.

Canadian Psychological Association (CPA) (www.cpa.ca): CPA's website provides a searchable directory of registered psychologists across Canada. You can narrow your search by location and specialty, including trauma and abuse.

Canadian Counselling and Psychotherapy Association (CCPA) (www.ccpa-accp.ca): CCPA offers a "Find a Professional" tool that helps you locate certified counselors and psychotherapists by province and specialty, including trauma and gender-based violence.

Ontario Association of Consultants, Counsellors, Psychometrists, and Psychotherapists (OACCPP) (www.oaccpp.ca): OACCPP offers a "Find a Practitioner" directory to help you locate professionals, including psychotherapists and counselors, in Ontario.

Psychology Foundation of Canada (PFC) (www.psychologyfoundation.org): PFC's website provides information on psychology services and resources, which can help you in your search for a therapist.

Canadian Mental Health Association (CMHA) (www.cmha.ca): CMHA has local branches across Canada that may offer counseling and support services for survivors of trauma and gender-based violence.

Therapist Locator by the American Psychological Association (APA) (www.apa.org): While this is primarily a U.S.-based resource, it may include international psychologists. You can search for therapists by location and specialty.

GoodTherapy (www.goodtherapy.org): GoodTherapy offers a directory of therapists worldwide. You can search by location and specify your preferences for therapists who specialize in trauma, abuse, or gender-related issues.

The International Society for Traumatic Stress Studies (ISTSS) (www.istss.org): ISTSS is a global organization focused on trauma-related issues. Their "Find a Clinician" directory can help you locate therapists with expertise in trauma treatment.

International Society for the Study of Trauma and Dissociation (ISSTD) (www.isst-d.org): ISSTD offers a directory of clinicians with expertise in the treatment of trauma and dissociation.

EMDR International Association (EMDRIA) (www.emdria.org): If you're interested in Eye Movement Desensitization and Reprocessing (EMDR) therapy, EMDRIA offers a directory of EMDR-certified therapists worldwide.

BetterHelp (www.betterhelp.com) and **Talkspace** (www.talkspace.com): These online therapy platforms offer access to licensed therapists, and you can often specify your preferences for therapists experienced in trauma and gender-based violence.

Flowing River Therapy (flowingrivertherapy.com) Offers in-person and online Yoga Therapy from certified Yoga Therapist Martha Mills.

Martha offers sliding scale trauma focused care for those healing from and living with anxiety, depression, PTSD, grief and loss, physical illness, and various forms of complex trauma such as, sexual assault, narcissistic abuse, and gender-based violence.

Online Counseling Platforms: There are various international online counseling platforms that connect individuals with licensed therapists. Some examples include 7 Cups, Regain, and Online-Therapy.com. Be sure to specify your needs when searching for a therapist.

Local Mental Health Organizations: Depending on your country or region, local mental health organizations and community clinics may offer therapy services and referrals to therapists experienced in trauma and gender-based violence.

When seeking a therapist, it's essential to do your research, interview potential therapists, and choose someone you feel comfortable with and who has the expertise to meet your specific needs. Remember that therapy can be a crucial part of healing for survivors of trauma and gender-based violence.

Community Support Groups:

Rituals for Recovery: Sisterhood Survivorship Support Group
https://ritualsforrecovery.com/help-her-recover-services

Offering hope and healing for those affected by sexualized violence and complex trauma. Survivorship is the process of coping with and managing the aftermath of a traumatic experience. When we come together, we learn we are not alone and the stories and wounds we carry can be dissolved. Through shared experiences and sacred conversation, our sisterhood support group provides a brave space to create new narratives, beliefs, and pathways to healing. In each session we explore a different topic around recovery, mental, emotional, and spiritual health.

It's confidential and inclusive to women survivors of all ages, races, ethnicities and backgrounds.

Healing Well: Healing Well offers online support communities for various health and wellness issues, including sexual abuse and domestic violence.

Psych Central Forums: Psych Central hosts forums on a wide range of mental health topics, including forums related to abuse and trauma recovery.

Pandora's Project (www.pandys.org): This online community and resource center offers support for survivors of sexual abuse and assault, including message boards, chat rooms, and articles.

NoMore.org: NoMore.org has an online community where survivors of domestic violence and sexual assault can connect and share their experiences.

SHE RECOVERS Foundation (www.sherecovers.org): This global nonprofit is focused on redefining recovery, inspiring hope, ending stigma and empowering women in or seeking recovery from mental health issues, trauma and substance use to increase their recovery capital, heal themselves and help other women to do the same.

Community Centers and Nonprofits: Check with community centers and nonprofits in your area, as they may host support groups for survivors of trauma and gender-based violence.

Religious and Spiritual Organizations: Some churches, mosques, synagogues, and other religious or spiritual organizations offer support groups for survivors within their communities.

Recovery Programs

Rituals for Recovery's https://ritualsforrecovery.com/our-programs

We help people heal from and build resilience to stress and trauma. We do this through the RFR Method, a "Trauma Responsive Mind-Body Wellness" (TRMBW™) model that heals trauma on all four levels - the physical, mental, emotional and energy body.

Rituals for Recovery (RfR) promotes mind-body wellness and social-emotional learning (SEL) by creating spaces for communities to learn and connect through mental health education and the healing arts. RfR trains educators, licensed healthcare professionals, community leaders, and employers on how to facilitate trauma-informed based discussions, become trauma-responsive, and create a culture of care within their organizations. We are proud to offer TRMBW™ & SEL training to individuals and organizations around the world!

HHR SEL(F): Help Her Recover, an arm of Rituals for Recovery, partners with social services, women's organizations, and local shelters to provide female victims of abuse, oppression, and family violence with access to trauma focused recovery support and mentorship. The Help Her Recover through Social-Emotional Learning for Femmes (HHR-SEL(F) Program equips women impacted by gender-based violence through peer to peer mentorship by matching survivors with our trained volunteer mentors. Together they embark on a year-long journey of healing through somatic mindfulness based social emotional learning (SEL), trauma informed care practices and training for complex trauma prevention.

Educational Initiatives and Workshops:

These programs are designed to raise awareness, provide education, and foster discussions on topics related to gender-based violence, consent, respect, and healthy relationships.

"Be A Voice Not an Echo" is an initiative created by Rituals for Recovery with a primary emphasis on tackling, ACES, gender-based violence and sexual assault within communities. Their collaborative efforts extend to schools, workplaces, and various organizations, aiming to elevate awareness, facilitate education, lower the occurrence of such incidents, and provide assistance to survivors. Through strategic partnerships, they jointly coordinate community events, awareness walks, rallies, and fundraising initiatives. Additionally, they craft educational resources through workshops, webinars, and seminars that center on topics such as ACES, gender-based violence, bystander intervention, and consent education.

Bringing in the Bystander: This program is designed to empower bystanders to intervene and prevent incidents of sexual and relationship violence. It teaches participants how to recognize signs of abuse and safely intervene in problematic situations.

Coaching Boys into Men: This program engages athletic coaches as positive role models for young athletes. It provides resources and training materials to help coaches teach their athletes about respect, consent, and healthy relationships.

Green Dot: The Green Dot program is another bystander intervention initiative aimed at preventing power-based personal violence, including sexual violence, dating violence, and stalking. It emphasizes the importance of individual actions in creating a safer community.

Love Is Not Abuse: This program, developed by the One Love Foundation, focuses on educating young people about healthy and unhealthy relationships. It provides workshops, videos, and other resources to help identify signs of abuse and promote respectful behavior.

Men Can Stop Rape: This organization offers workshops and training programs aimed at engaging men and boys in the prevention of gender-based violence. They focus on the role of men in promoting respect and ending violence against women.

RESPECT Program: Developed by the National Sexual Violence Resource Center (NSVRC), this program offers a range of educational resources and training materials to promote respectful behavior, consent, and healthy relationships.

Start Strong: This program targets middle school students and focuses on building healthy relationship skills, preventing dating violence, and promoting gender equity. It includes curriculum resources and training for educators.

The Fourth R: This evidence-based program is designed for schools and focuses on promoting healthy relationships and preventing dating violence among adolescents. It includes classroom lessons, interactive activities, and teacher training.

The Help Her Recover Project: The Help Her Recover Project is a call to action to address violence against women, demand equity and promote good health and wellbeing. **The Help Her Recover Project** will bring the message of awareness of the impact of trauma to Canadians through the publication of this book: Speak Out and Help Her Recover, a 12-month, high-profile awareness campaign across Canada, and a hybrid international conference.

Social Media Campaigns and Online Activism:

To engage with online campaigns and social media movements dedicated to raising awareness about gender-based violence and supporting survivors check out the United Nations Annual Campaign:

UNITE TO END VIOLENCE AGAINST WOMEN CAMPAIGN

16 Days of Activism - Unite/Orange the World Toolkit

https://www.unwomen.org/en/what-we-do/ending-violence-against-women/unite/toolkit?gclid=Cj0KCQjwpompBhDZARIsAFD_Fp_bKUPWN8zRzRl4zIRut4YAFTEWwIGsmr66YU68h-kUDVisxPS1jolkaAiGLEALw_wcB

TED Talks

These TED Talks provide valuable insights and inspiration for addressing gender-based violence and creating a more equitable and just world.

Leymah Gbowee: Unlock the Intelligence, Passion, Greatness of Girls: Nobel Laureate Leymah Gbowee discusses the power of girls and young women in preventing violence and conflict in their communities.

Kavita Ramdas: Radical Women, Embracing Tradition: Kavita Ramdas explores the ways in which women around the world are standing up against violence and oppression, often drawing from their cultural traditions to drive change.

Tony Porter: A Call to Men: Tony Porter discusses the need to redefine and challenge traditional masculinity to combat gender-based violence and create healthier relationships.

Morgana Bailey: The Danger of Hiding Who You Are: Morgana Bailey shares her personal journey of coming out as gay and the connection between self-acceptance and ending discrimination and violence.

Sheryl WuDunn: Our Century's Greatest Injustice: Sheryl WuDunn discusses the global issue of gender-based violence and its connection to poverty and lack of education, highlighting the importance of empowering women.

Leslie Morgan Steiner: Why Domestic Violence Victims Don't Leave: Leslie Morgan Steiner shares her personal experience with domestic violence and explores the complex reasons why many victims stay in abusive relationships.

Aqeela Sherrills: Violence Interrupters: Aqeela Sherrills discusses his work as a violence interrupter in Los Angeles and how communities can come together to prevent violence.

Eve Ensler: Embrace Your Inner Girl: Playwright and activist Eve Ensler encourages women to embrace their inner girl and reconnect with their strength and resilience in the face of violence.

Zainab Salbi: Women, Wartime, and the Dream of Peace: Zainab Salbi shares stories of women from conflict zones around the world and their role in working towards peace and justice.

Jackson Katz: Violence Against Women — It's a Men's Issue: Jackson Katz explores the role of men in preventing violence against women and emphasizes the importance of men taking responsibility for their actions and attitudes.

Podcasts

There are several podcasts that address the issue of ending gender-based violence, provide support for survivors, and promote awareness and education. Here are some podcasts that focus on this important topic:

"What Works" - Hosted by Tara McMullin, this podcast explores various aspects of ending gender-based violence, including conversations with experts, survivors, and advocates. It covers topics like domestic violence, sexual assault, and related issues.

"Voices of Hope" - This podcast features stories of hope, resilience, and healing from survivors of gender-based violence. It provides a platform for survivors to share their experiences and insights.

"The #MeToo Movement" - This podcast delves into the #MeToo movement and its impact on society. It includes discussions about sexual harassment, assault, and the broader conversation surrounding consent and respect.

"The Domestic Violence Discussion" - Hosted by Advocate Melinda Salzman, this podcast raises awareness about domestic violence and provides resources for survivors. It includes interviews with experts and survivors sharing their stories.

"The Healing Place Podcast" - This podcast focuses on trauma, healing, and resilience, including topics related to gender-based violence. It features interviews with experts and survivors discussing various healing modalities.

"What We Don't Talk About" - Hosted by Jo Robertson, this podcast explores topics that are often considered taboo, including gender-based violence. It includes interviews with survivors, advocates, and experts in the field.

"The Survivor's Guide to Life" - This podcast provides support and guidance for survivors of trauma, including gender-based violence. It covers topics like healing, self-care, and personal growth.

"The Consent Guidebook" - Hosted by Katherine Druckman, this podcast focuses on consent education and discussions surrounding consent, boundaries, and respect in relationships.

"The Incest Diary" - This podcast, based on the book of the same name by Anonymous, delves into the survivor's experience of incest and its long-lasting impact. It explores themes of trauma, healing, and resilience.

"Not Your Fault" - This podcast aims to reduce the stigma around sexual assault and create a supportive space for survivors to share their stories. It features interviews with survivors and experts.

"After Dark Podcast" - This podcast Interviews survivors of domestic violence so they can share their story and inspire others.

You can easily find these podcasts on popular podcast platforms such as Apple Podcasts, Spotify, Google Podcasts, or by visiting the official websites of the podcast hosts or organizations associated with the podcasts.

ACKNOWLEDGEMENTS

The creation of this book, *Speak Out and Help Her Recover*, has been a journey of immense courage, resilience, and collaboration. We would like to take a moment to express our deepest gratitude to the incredible individuals and organizations who have made this project possible.

To the Survivors: Your unwavering strength, vulnerability, and willingness to share your stories have illuminated the path toward healing and empowerment. Your voices are the heart and soul of this book, and we are endlessly inspired by your bravery.

To the Contributors: Our sincere appreciation goes out to the writers, editors, artists, and all those who lent their talents to shape these narratives into a powerful collective voice. Your dedication to amplifying these stories is immeasurable.

To the Advocates and Organizations: We extend our heartfelt thanks to the advocates, support organizations, and community leaders who tirelessly work to end gender-based violence. Your commitment to change and your ongoing support for survivors are the driving force behind this movement.

To the Readers: Your engagement and willingness to listen, learn, and act are vital to the continued progress in addressing gender-based violence. Your presence in this journey is a beacon of hope.

To Friends and Family: Your unwavering support, encouragement, and understanding have sustained us throughout this endeavor. Your belief in our mission has been a constant source of inspiration.

To the Healers: We acknowledge the therapists, counselors, and mental health professionals who guide survivors on their journey to recovery. Your expertise and compassion are essential in the healing process.

To the Communities: Our gratitude goes to the communities that stand in solidarity against gender-based violence. Your collective strength has the power to bring about real change.

To the Authors: Your dedication to sharing these stories with the world has created a platform for hope, healing, and change. Your commitment to shedding light on these important issues is commendable.

To Our Supporters: We extend our appreciation to those who have offered financial support, resources, and encouragement. Your contributions have been instrumental in making this project a reality.

To the Future: We look forward to a world where gender-based violence is a thing of the past. May this book serve as a testament to the strength of survivors and a call to action for a safer, more compassionate world.

In unity and solidarity, we move forward, armed with stories of hope and healing, determined to create lasting change.

With deepest gratitude,

Amanda Willett
Founder Rituals for Recovery, The Help Her Recover Project

ABOUT AMANDA WILLETT

Amanda Willett is the founder of Rituals for Recovery and a survivor of complex trauma. She is a dedicated advocate for ending Gender-Based Violence (GBV) and promoting trauma-informed practices. Amanda's vision is to create a trauma-responsive world, and her commitment to healing led her to publish *Speak Out and Help Her Recover,* marking the first step in her transformative mission.

Amanda provides invaluable support through consultations, workshops, mentoring, and program development, specializing in trauma-informed and culturally responsive guidance. Her expertise has earned her recognition as a changemaker in the prestigious 2022 international coffee table book, *Who's Who of the World.*

As a social entrepreneur, recovery coach, and global inspiration, Amanda focuses on creating trauma-responsive communities worldwide. She advocates for human rights, offering international training and organizational coaching to hospitals, schools, and social service agencies.

Amanda is a renowned expert in the RfR Method, empowering helping professionals with trauma-responsive skills to support individuals on their journey to recovery from long-term stress and trauma.

With over two decades of diverse experience, Amanda is a dynamic influencer dedicated to helping survivors of GBV and complex trauma regain their dignity and rebuild their lives. She passionately raises awareness about the impact of trauma on lifelong health, emphasizing the Adverse Childhood Experiences (ACEs) and Positive Childhood Experiences (PCEs) studies.

Amanda's leadership and innovation have earned her recognition, and she is committed to helping others succeed. She mentors and inspires individuals through speaking engagements for women's groups, corporations, and non-profits worldwide.

Under Amanda's leadership, Rituals for Recovery received a nomination for Non-Profit of the Year by the Whitby Chamber of Commerce. She was also nominated as the G100 Canada Country Chair for Human Rights and featured as a 2022 Awardee in the international coffee table book "Who's Who of the World."

Education is a cornerstone of Amanda's mission. She holds a diploma in Business Administration and Human Resource Management from Durham College and completed her Workplace Mental Health Leadership certificate through Queens University. Amanda is a member of Yoga Alliance and has received multiple yoga and somatic healing teacher training certificates, including 200-hour yoga teacher training certificate through Soul Work™, 300-hour yoga psychology teacher training certificate with Ashley Turner, Trauma Informed Yoga Training with Ashley Turner, Yoga Nidra Teacher Training with Yoga Fit, and Mindfulness Resilience Training with Veterans Yoga Project. She is also currently completing the Art of Rest, Restorative and YIN YTT by Scott Davis, and the Heart Math Clinical Certification for Stress, Anxiety, and Emotional Regulation.

As a trauma recovery coach, Amanda specializes in providing trauma relief tools for self-nurture, assisting survivors in managing mental health challenges. Her approach combines psycho-educational tools, therapeutic interventions, and evidence-based self-regulation techniques, rooted in yoga, energy work, Jungian psychology, and positive psychology.

Amanda believes that joy and wellbeing are fundamental human rights. Rituals for Recovery reflects her passionate belief in self-reclamation's transformative power to heal individuals and the world through compassion, understanding, and resilience.

www.ingramcontent.com/pod-product-compliance
Lightning Source LLC
Chambersburg PA
CBHW071333080526
44587CB00017B/2826